X1

D0361778

Toxic Mom Toolkit

Discovering a Happy Life Despite Toxic Parenting

By Rayne Wolfe

Copyright © 2013 Rayne Wolfe
All rights reserved.
ISBN: 1492782386
ISBN 13: 9781492782384
Library of Congress Control Number: 2013917430
CreateSpace Independent Publishing Platform
North Charleston, South Carolina

Dedication

To my husband, Aristotle Wolfe,
the first person in my life that *got it*.

A note on the organization of this book:

This book includes my memoir, stories of other women who grew up with Toxic Moms, tools you can use and self-tests. The upper right hand corner of the first page of each chapter will indicate (my) **Memoir,** (other) **Voices, Tools** or **Self-Test** to help orient the reader.

Each **VOICES** entry is based on a twenty-question survey completed by a real person. Each person is identified by an initial and year of birth. When possible, information on country of origin is included. My own completed questionnaire is included at the end of the book.

Toxic Mom Toolkit
By Rayne Wolfe

Table of Contents

# # #

CHAPTER ONE
The End Of Secrets

MEMOIR

*H*ow many times on lunch breaks, coffee dates or over drinks had I listened to girlfriends worry aloud about their moms getting older?

One friend chewed her fingernails over her mother's diminishing memory, eyesight and balance. She worried the bite of Midwest winters and her mother's growing isolation was a formula for a 3 a.m. call from the police, or a hospital or worse. Her mother would never move west. Not at her age. Would my friend have to uproot her family and change jobs in order to move closer to her mother?

I let my friends vent about their moms and patted their forearms across the table. Did they ever suspect that I did not truly share their concerns? When they asked about my mother I always said she was good. She lived ten minutes away in a very nice seniors home and was very, very independent.

I was lucky, they said. Their mothers expected so much from them. Their mothers demanded weekly visits and holiday get-togethers. Mine knew I was a busy newspaper reporter, I said.

What my friends didn't know then was that the mother I was referring to was my stepmother Robbie, the witty and well-traveled dame who was my dad's second wife after my parents divorced. My stepmother was my third mother, the easy-breezy one who redeemed mothering for me.

Only a handful of friends knew that I had a birth mother, let's call her "Virginia," who variously described my conception as a "date rape thing," a "terrible time," and the one thing in her life she wished never happened. I never told anyone the worst thing I heard about my origins. Extended members of my birth family had told me that I might be the product of incest between Virginia and her father.

Only a tight circle of friends knew that my adoptive mother, Norm, who raised me from three-weeks old to the day I turned 18 *and not a minute longer* hadn't been much a part of my life since my mid-twenties when I began curtailing contact.

In my twenties I identified my birth mother who when I first contacted her by phone denied she was my mother then quickly pleaded that we just "forget the whole deal." "Some boy," (or maybe her own father), or her fiancé raped her; she couldn't remember. Really, who cared anyway?

My birth mother was one of five sisters and one brother raised on an Iowa farm. As adults, several of the sisters earned wild reputations for neglecting their own children. For example, one aunt got in trouble with the law for leaving two toddlers in a motel room so she could go off drinking, a distant cousin told me.

My adoptive mother, Norm, was such a lousy mother in so many ways for her entire life that it's just hard to explain. If she wasn't breaking wooden spoons on us, she was threatening to sell us to the gypsies. I sometimes feel that I didn't so much reject my mother as I survived her.

My third mother was my adorable stepmother, who nursed my dad through three years of brain cancer including two surgeries until his death in 1996. She's the one who introduced me to fabulous places like the San Francisco Ballet, American Conservatory Theater and Gump's. She gave me real gold jewelry and with a wink told me not to lose it. She was the "mother" my husband and I happily looked out for as she entered her frail seniority and elderly decline.

After a lifetime of abuse, neglect, dishonesty and craziness, by my thirties, I had let my relationship with my adoptive mother go completely. I had to.

When friends spoke of their mothers I sometimes felt ashamed of my broken bonds with my own birth mother and adoptive mother. I could care less about Sunday calls. I had no holiday plans with my family. I was not concerned about my mother's doctors' appointments. I did not drive her anywhere, nor was I required to pick her up. The idea would never occur to me.

I had a secret: I was the daughter of not one, but two, toxic mothers.

I could justify my decision to my husband, to my brother, and to an inner circle of close friends. When my father was still alive, the rift between his ex-wife and daughter bothered him. Several times he cornered me in his kitchen to press: All moms and teen daughters fight. What on earth could make me so mad at my mother? I told him I wasn't mad, I was just done. He seemed to be convinced that we had had one epic fight. Certainly enough time had gone by to bury the hatchet, hadn't it?

Explaining why I felt the way I did would only have hurt my father deeply. I didn't want him to hear the details of what happened to me in my mother's care. I didn't want him to visualize any of it. He already felt guilty enough for the divorce. Plus, I suspected my father was capable of being one of those Greatest Generation guys who would listen quietly and over the next few days get his affairs in order and then go shoot someone.

At first, rejecting who I thought of as my own mother, the mother who raised me, was a terribly hard decision to live with. It involved secrets and silence and wondering what others would think.

It put me in a position made all the more difficult considering that my mother was a life-long mystery to just about everyone. She was secretive and led a vivid fantasy life that sometimes bled into reality. She had so many clandestine romances that I think she had trouble keeping all the players straight. Her life was exciting and dangerous and sexy – *in her head*. From my perspective it was dishonest, slatternly and sad.

Everyone grows up, and as I matured sufficiently to compare my life to the life my mother led at the same age - - lining us up side by side in our twenties, our thirties - - I came to realize that my decision to cut her off was the only sane option.

Too bad she didn't feel the same way. Like a scab that never heals, she would pick at the broken relationship, sending gushy birthday cards or showing up unexpectedly at social gatherings. Every phone call, note or sighting was emotionally draining for me.

When I was younger, I was defiant trying my best to be very tough about cutting contact with my mother. As I matured, I chose to be as kind as possible without appearing weak or receptive. By the time I was in my early forties, I was pretty good at having a no-contact toxic mom. I'm still amazed that my husband married me without ever meeting my mother. Our yearlong engagement commenced just when my father was informed he would die of brain cancer. Suddenly, every moment was so precious. I felt like I had this little tiny window for my father and my soon-to-be husband to learn to appreciate one another. Time is too short not to focus on the good.

Six weeks before our wedding, just before he died my father made me promise not to delay happiness; not to let the sadness of losing someone I loved defer me from loving my husband with all my heart. After two surgeries to remove tumors, his vocabulary was simple.

"He loves you. You love him. Just be happy. If you're happy for five years you're way ahead of most people," he said.

We enjoyed our first five years together, then ten, now we're at 15 plus. Life went on.

I've never been a whiner. So don't expect any whining here.

By the time I was in my forties, it got to a point where, in a room of 20 women, I could spot the two or three that shared my toxic mom secret. In conversations we could finish each other's sentences. We'd wave one another off when childhood memories conjured up anger or sadness. We guffawed at stories of neglect and housewifely threats to small children. We traded stories of unique punishments, trying to one-up each other. I suspected that daughters of toxic mothers were a large silent group of interesting women willing to talk about it if someone just asked.

I became a newspaper reporter. A reporter is conditioned to notice patterns that lead to stories. I began slowly collecting friends' stories about awful mothers. In a newsroom they call this "gathering string." Some reporters will gather snippets for years before they have enough to knit together to make an interesting story. Often the timing has to be right. It helps if a cataclysmic world event helps prove the theory. Mass shootings are good to tack on family issues stories.

So I waited.

I didn't know what I could do with these stories of nice and happy women who survived their own spectacularly horrible mothers. Yet I was convinced that the aggregation of this type of wisdom could help others in the future. It wasn't until I finished writing my entire book that I realized all I wanted to do was give other women permission to say, "My mother was a horrible mother," out loud and not feel that somehow they deserved such horrible treatment.

I have learned that not every adult daughter or son needs to or wants to make a complete break from a toxic mom. Some make rules and limit contact. Others refuse to let their mothers near their own children. Some put up with their mothers in order to keep tabs on other family members like younger siblings or their dads. Only a few of the daughters of toxic mothers were like me. Done.

What kind of a mother was my mother?

Well, she *did* take me everywhere with her.

She took me to her married boyfriends' homes, and on weekend romps with married bosses and to smoky neighborhood bars where I was left at the curb locked in her turquoise Chevy Impala with a cotton pillow slip to embroider for up to three, four, or five hours. I was told that if I opened the door or rolled down the window she would know when she got back and I'd be in T-R-O-U-B-L-E.

The grammar school me sat eye-to-eye with the glove box button. I'd put down my sewing and gaze up to study the black telephone lines slicing the gray sky and then back down at the long chains of tiny, perfect stitches my little fingers had wrought. Looking up and down while sitting in a plastic bucket seat super-charged my long fine hair with static electricity. I think it's why in so many childhood photos I look like I just ran in from a storm.

So, you can imagine how close my mother and I were.

TOOLS

**"To succeed it is necessary to accept
the world as it is and rise above it."
– Michael Korda**

YOUR INVISIBLE CROWN

Never leave the house without your invisible crown.

By imagining ourselves wearing royal crowns, we become monarchs of our emotions and develop the discipline to create our ideal and peaceful lives.

Whether you prefer sparkling jewels or feathers or pink felt, imagine your perfect crown and place it atop your head as you head out into the world each day. You are royal and kind, patient and welcoming and you are deserving of royal treatment in return. Design your crown and own it.

CHAPTER TWO
School Clothes

MEMOIR

*T*he Richmond District streets of San Francisco were extra wide and heaven sent for days filled with roller-skating and riding bikes. In front of some houses the concrete sparkled with imbedded crushed glass while other decorative sections marking off driveways were painted brick red or "Park and Rec" green, perfect for "race ya!" turnaround points.

A block from our shotgun flat, Golden Gate Park lured us with fragrant plumes of pine pollen coursing through the air, pushed and pulled by electric streetcars whooooooshing on the Fulton Street line. The park was our playground and infused our clothes with scents of damp bark and freshly mown grass, smells that knitted well with the salty sea air rolling up from Ocean Beach.

Nearly every morning was a foggy morning. I'd steal a few delicious minutes snuggling down into my still warm bed; listening to dew dropping off the eaves and the backyard fence creaking as it swelled with moisture. Robins pierced the gray dawn with jazzy calls that made me giggle.

The city had a dozen foghorns then blasting "Beee-Oooooo" all night long to direct ships through the Golden Gate. Before the sun could burn off the damp, stone steps were slick, sidewalks were soaked and even little kids knew better than to dash when worn leather bottomed shoes could so easily fly out from under them.

Maybe it's just because I grew up in the avenues, but I'm almost always cold now. In Hawaii I still wrap a cotton scarf around my neck. At an outdoor pool on the most scorching Indian summer day, I still require the thickest, warmest towels. The fuzziest slippers require thick socks, preferably knee length: In the winter, preferably cashmere. No doubt I'll be one of those old ladies I've interviewed a million times with the windows caulked shut and the wall heater blasting. I too, will have my own water bottle-shaped dog looking up at visitors with pleading eyes begging to be rescued.

The room in which I am most cold is always the bathroom. I dread undressing and stepping into a hot shower for that nano-second before the reassuringly hot water warms my skin. My face crinkles up like a newborn ready to cry. Every shower is too short. I hold my breath between a furious dry off and leap into an ankle-length fleece robe.

When I was tiny, my family began driving north on weekends with friends to enjoy Scandinavian-style health spas. That's where I was dropped into the deep end of a cold pool with good-natured exhortations to move or drown. Luckily for me, I was hard-wired to love splashing and swimming. I might be my calmest in the roughest water having survived river-rafting fall-outs, being pulled out to sea by under-tows in Hawaii and once having been sucked underneath a fallen tree on the Snake River.

If we could afford it, we would drive up to Calistoga or Sonoma and spend summer weekends at a spa with an outdoor pool and indoor saunas, massage and treatment rooms. My brother had asthma so we generally chose places that had a eucalyptus sauna. Saunas that used botanicals usually had a red light bulb inside that made everyone inside look as pink as a bottle of Pepto Bismol.

I stuck to the pool. My parents used to feed me lunch on the lip of the pool, in the water up to my armpits, because it was easier than the argument required to drag me out crying. You could drop me into any lake, a river, the ocean, a creek, or a friend's pool and forget about me. You could hand me a towel and money for a Fudgsicle at noon and stay in a bar till six.

You'd think my mother would have been more careful at home where there was no lifeguard or other parents around. After all we had a relative whose toddler son had drowned in a backyard pool. Yet my mother would plop me in a lukewarm bath up to my shoulders, toss me a washcloth and disappear. Maybe she was hoping I'd drown. Too bad for her I was such a little fish.

Bath time was alone time. I had no expectation that my mother would stay in the bathroom with me. There was no playing or talking. There were no suds, no toys, although I do remember rubber-paged books with circus elephants and trained seals that I could "read" under water. I taught myself that when the bath water really got cold, to climb out for a few seconds and jump back in. The quick chill from the air made the water feel warmer because you were a little bit colder. You could do that a few times but eventually, it was far too cold to stay in.

On Indian summer days up in the country, I was a champ at warming up by lying on the cement deck around the pool to soak up the heat. But in our little apartment, left too long in the tub, I'd make my way to the little square metal grill set into the floorboards. Heat cost money, so it didn't run regularly. But I'd wait, shaking with wet hair, for a rare blast from the furnace.

Remember those old cartoons when all that children can see are the adult's shoes and legs just up to the knees? That's how my world felt to me then. I was so little and I didn't understand why legs appeared or disappeared. I had no hope of making them appear when I needed them. For some reason I never screamed or cried or demanded legs fix things for me. I just did my best. The best a three- or four- or five-year-old could do under the circumstances.

In managing not to drown or die of pneumonia, eventually I was old enough to attend public school.

My mother briskly showed me the route: one block down, one over and one up. Really, all you needed to do was stand still and follow the roaring noise of the schoolyard less than two blocks from our flat. The street in front of our school was a four-lane speedway that bisected our neighborhood and led to the Golden Gate Bridge.

My brother, who was five years older, took me to school at first, but at some point was deemed an unreliable escort. My mother arranged for a neighborhood girl to swing by our house each weekday morning to walk me to school. It was 1963 and girls wore knee length dresses with anklets and Buster Brown leather soled shoes. One day I confided to the big girl that I was cold. Bless her heart she offered me her sweater, but I was still cold. "I'm so cold, I'm so cold, I'm so cold," I chanted with teeth chattering. At the school gate she discovered my chilling problem. I had left the house without underpants.

We quickly retraced our steps while I held down my dress and the older girl wrapped her arm around my shoulders protectively.

I remember my mother was annoyed by the unexpected interruption. She was on the phone and would have to hang up. It was obvious she was mad at me for being so stupid and causing her to cut a conversation short.

"Who leaves the house like that?" she kept saying.

My mother always told me that I got my underwear dirty on purpose. She decided that she could reduce laundry *and* teach me a lesson by giving me just one pair of panties per week. She didn't care if wearing soiled underclothes caused boils on my bottom. Kids get boils, she said. If I soiled my underpants, or had an accident in them, that was my problem. I also lived in dread of anyone catching a glimpse of my ugly underpants. The elastic was always stretched out and they were so dingy and gray. I hated wearing pairs that had spots that wouldn't wash out.

Today my panties are folded neatly and laid out by color in a lavender sachet-scented drawer. Because I live in the Wine County I'm able to grow and harvest my own lavender and make the sachets. It is a summer project I look forward to. I also make it a point to share bags of lavender with friends to tuck in their closets and drawers. I can reach into a drawer and easily choose a fresh pair of silken panties that will compliment any one of a dozen lovely brassieres. I love doing laundry. I love folding my clothes and putting them away. I love ironing and mending and take great comfort in knowing that my clothes are always fresh and clean.

On that morning, my three pairs of dirty underpants were all in the dirty laundry bin on the back porch. The older girl waited in the living room while I was marched back to the tiny laundry area behind our kitchen. My mother fished out a dirty pair and spanked me as she forced my shoes through the leg openings, pulling the cotton along the wet soles.

"What…. IS…. the….. matter…. with…. YOU?" she chanted as she struggled to simultaneously swat me and dress me.

As my mother sent us on our way for the second time the girl asked my mother if I could also have a sweater. My teeth were chattering again.

"She'll just lose it. She'll be perfectly fine once she's in the school," my mother said shooing us out the front door.

CHAPTER THREE
The Toxic Tyrant

VOICES

**"I know some of my neighbors
better than I know my mom."**
- H, born 1954

She is one of seven siblings and the oldest daughter. Her parents met in January of 1946 when her mother was 21 and her father was 25. They married in July and had their first son precisely nine months later.

"My mother was a homemaker. My dad... he was a salesman I guess. He sold everything. He sold furniture, tires. At the end, he sold real estate," she said.

The family moved so often that H can count twelve schools during her K through 12 years. Her father said he liked to move.

What none of the children knew was that their father had a secret. He was one of millions of Depression-era children shipped off as a boy to live with his extended family. "Unfortunately, that's where he was molested by a male family member."

"That whole generation from the Depression through WWII, I think they missed something in their upbringing or in their genes. They are so distant," H said.

Unsuccessful in life, the parents compensated by running the home like a spit and polish boot camp. Orders were issued. Chores were completed quickly, without any lip. The children were not allowed to sleep over at friends' homes, nor were school friends brought home. None of the children ever challenged their parents.

"I feared my parents. I knew they would kill me if I did anything wrong," she recalled.

As a youngster H regarded her father mainly as stern and aloof. She considered her mother a tyrant. As a teenager, she decided her mother was a stupid tyrant.

"She was incredulous I could breathe. Constant belittling. She'd ask me my weight and then say, 'Well, you look every ounce of it,'" she remembers.

In this age of constant building up, with *My Child is a Superstar!* bumper stickers on every PTA member's mini-van, it's hard to believe H's mother instilled doubts in her children at every opportunity.

Instead of saying, "Have a good day!" she would send her daughter off each morning with a "You're not wearing *that* to school are you?" dig.

My mom thought we were little reflections of her, and she hated herself so much she couldn't love us," she said.

One guess why H's mother hated herself.

"My mother was molested at age three. She was overweight as a teen tipping the scales at 183 and only 5 foot 3 inches tall."

Both of H's mother's parents (H's grandparents) were alcoholics and did nothing more than menial work. Her mother's mother was particularly verbally and physically abusive. In her mom's senior year of high school, she dieted her way to a new look. Then the slimmed down 18-year-old developed a hatred for fat people.

"My mother taught us that fat people are stupid people."

A relative told H that after high school her mother was offered a scholarship to art school, but turned it down saying that she couldn't afford the bus fares to and from the campus.

"I had no clue that my mother was a very good artist and was a good singer. When she married my dad she put all her desires and dreams away. She was very depressed," said H.

H's mother was so shut down that she never wanted to learn to drive a car. She never wrote a check. She would make out a grocery list and her husband, who apparently lived in fear of his children being molested, made quick trips to the market. That way an adult was always present in the home.

She can't recall any calm discussions with either parent. No giggles over sudsy dishes. No chatting on the porch swing and listening to crickets. No inside jokes. No silly traditions. No tears gently wiped. No dreaming together.

Her mother never told H she was loved, nor did her father.

"When I was a teenager, I started noticing how other mothers and daughters had conversations and got along and did things for each other. I became jealous of friends who had good relationships with their moms," she said. "My mother couldn't wait for us to grow up and move out."

School was a refuge for this daughter. With a little college and a lot of hard work she earned a high-ranking civil service job for the Office of Education. She married rather young and, luckily, she married the right man - a good man. Together they had two sons. One is a successful musician. The other enjoys his career in law enforcement. The sons adore their mother and enjoy seeing her as often as possible inviting her to all the benchmarks in their lives. In every family photo she's smiling.

She remembers her goal while pregnant with her first son. She wanted to create a loving and nurturing environment. That was the most important thing in the world for her.

"I made sure he knew that I loved him every minute of every day. I spent time on the floor with him, something my mother never did," she said. "When our second son came along I did the same for him. I loved him to pieces."

About twenty years ago, out of the blue, she stopped receiving invitations to family events. Her parents had decided to cut her out of their lives. She was being punished for stating the obvious about her parents to her siblings. While the older ones shared her experience and were sympathetic, one of H's younger siblings thought all the toxic parenting talk was mainly her imagination.

"I really didn't wish them any harm. I mourned losing my dad a little bit although he was a huge part of the problem… (When they cut me off) I praised God that they had nothing to do with me. I felt such freedom."

In 2009, when her father was dying of pancreatic cancer, he summoned all seven of his adult children to his hospital bedside. At that time he was estranged from one son and three daughters, including H.

"We all went to see him and he was all, how's the weather? He never said he loved any one of us," she said.

She finds talking to friends about her parents, especially her mother, very difficult. There are only one or two close friends with whom she can talk frankly about her relationship with her mother.

"They have good relationships with their mothers and worry about me. But they listen and they don't judge me," she said.

She feels fortunate that she has been able to transplant her mother "from the emotional side of her brain, to the logical side." She can stand back now and look at her parents as people with sad pasts and problems. She has not felt the need to talk to a therapist about it.

"I can't see myself helping her in the future. I know some of my neighbors better than I know my mom."

A busy, family-focused mom and successful administrator, she feels no guilt or remorse for her decision to let others look after her widowed mother in her waning years.

"I feel that I understand what she went through. That she never changed or matured or worked things out is not my fault," she said. "Going forward she is the one missing out on things she doesn't know exists."

A note from H 1954:

I am just about to retire and move to Hawaii. We are very excited about our new life—but I am not certain if I can be that far away from my children. If it is too far away, we will come back. It is very important to me to be a part of my kids' lives. I may have grandchildren one day…and I would love to be involved in their lives.

 My relationship with my mother is unchanged. While she has spoken to other family members about her regret of our current situation, she has done nothing to change things. I am still perfectly happy with our relationship. I made peace with it so many years ago.

CHAPTER FOUR
Call Out The Gurkhas

MEMOIR

*J*en and I were having our monthly Eggs Benedict brunch (my eggs hard as golf balls, hers not so much) when she asked me what I'd do if I won the lottery. The newspaper headlines were trumpeting a huge jackpot.

I happen to have given this a lot of thought. I've even written out my "to do" list, should my winning numbers come up. In previous daydreams I had concluded that it all comes down to world travel. Say you win $100 million. First you pay your bills, and then you pay the bills of those you love. Then you buy a house or two and have some shared experiences with loved ones to recall with a sigh when you're old and in a wheelchair. But after that shower of riches, it really boils down to the ability to go see whatever you want.

The Vatican on Easter Sunday? Amen. Front row seats at the Paris Opera, gazing at the shimmering Aurora Borealis in Norway or the running of the bulls in Pamplona? Easy-breezy-peezy – with millions.

Jen agreed I had a point. So where would I go with my Lotto winnings she wanted to know.

"Oh, I wouldn't go anywhere, that's for normal people. What I'd do is build a small suite onto our house and hire a Gurkha houseman," I said. *"I've wanted a Gurkha houseman in a white jacket all my life."*

Nepalese Gurkha's have fought alongside the British for hundreds of years and are considered among the bravest and most loyal fighting men on earth. When they retire from military service many work as bodyguards or house managers to those with security concerns, I explained as I tested the denseness of my egg yolk.

Jen's eyes bugged out.

As a fellow toxic mom enthusiast, she knew that any story blurted out like that certainly had something to do with my toxic mother. She grabbed the edge of the marble café table and demanded, *"Tell!"*

When I was little and the doorbell rang at our San Francisco flat my mother would grab me from behind – one arm around my tiny waist and the other over my mouth – and clutch me to her own chest, dragging me backwards to the hall coat closet. She'd inch deeper into the space quieter than a cat to hunch in a corner behind the second-hand vacuum cleaner.

Is there anything worse than seeing nothing when your eyes are wide open in fear? With our faces smushed against musty woolen coats we'd wait until the coast was clear.

Yeah, I know. Who's mother does this even once?

As an adult I can guess she was afraid of something. Was the rent overdue? Was my mother avoiding man complications? Was it the truant officer? I'll never know for sure. But I do know for the little kid who still resides in my brain: Nothing is scarier than a doorbell.

Not too long after I confessed my doorbell/closet story to Jen, The Mister and I bought our current house. Married for eight years, it wasn't until we moved into the new house that my husband realized I avoided answering the door. He asked me why. (Dang, he's so logical!)

Learning that I was carrying around my mother's inexplicable fear of doorbells he threatened to devise a regime of nearly constant random doorbell ringing and to time me on my responses. He would brief and encourage neighbors and friends to pop in as often as possible.

What might be a two- to three-minute ordeal of looking out windows, through peepholes and smelling the crack for danger would be whittled down to one super charged moment of dread as I flung open our front door expecting to be impaled with a rusty pitchfork. Yes, perhaps he could desensitize me, but truth be told, I'd still pay someone to greet visitors.

Lotto gods willing, I'll hire my own Gurkha.

You never know, one day it could be my birth mother on my stoop and I'll be glad there's a hired killer in my employ between us.

CHAPTER FIVE
Dreaming About A Normal Life

VOICES

"I would watch the women at these mirrors, always putting on make up and going through this one door. My mother told me to never open that door."

- K born 1979

I was sitting in jail. On the other side of the bulletproof glass was a young woman with black waist-length hair. Incarcerated for two years while awaiting trial she was facing a possible 30-year sentence. Dreading a crucial court date, she nevertheless agreed to talk to me about her toxic mother.

The inmate's mother came from a good family in Thailand, a rich family. The mother had arrived in America with a much older husband and a passport that said she was 18 although she was actually 14. K's mother was also eight months pregnant. K is now 30 and goes by a typical high school cheerleader's name, instead of her ethnic birth name.

Not that she actually attended high school. By 14 K ran away to join her wandering mother in Texas where she was living in the back of a strip mall massage parlor.

"I would watch the women at these mirrors, always putting on make up and going through this one door. My mother told me to never open that door," she said.

Of course the daughter became a prostitute. Of course drug addiction followed. And, yes, she became pregnant. In jail, she attends drug school and works toward her GED. In jail, she works on improving her English vocabulary. In jail, she's dreaming of a normal life.

"When I was pregnant I was thinking of nice things for my daughter. It was the first time I thought I could never do what my mother did to me," she said.

She reads and re-reads poems her own 13-year-old daughter writes. She never shows them to other inmates. They're too personal.

"That would be like handing them bullets. Ammunition to hurt me with," she said with a shrug.

The young woman in jail was taught by her mother that it was better to sleep with strangers and make money than to sleep with boys her own age and be poor. By 15 she was wearing nice clothes, buying solid gold jewelry and driving a car from state to state to work as a massage parlor hooker.

She's not stupid. She speaks four languages fluently. Despite her lack of education she always knew something wasn't right.

"My mother would introduce me to her customers as her daughter and I'd say, 'Mom that sounds so bad. Say I'm your cousin.'"

I looked at her through the glass with my jaw dropped open. She nodded, smiling.

Nobody ever told this jail inmate that her mother was a bad influence. Growing up, the only people this girl ever met were customers and other sex workers, some even younger than she. Averaging three customers an hour, her breaks were spent watching bootleg videos of a popular Thai soap opera.

"I watched that show so long that the actresses that were girls my age then are the mothers in the show now," she said with a smile.

❧ ❧

I was afraid gathering these toxic mom stories would be hard. What I thought was the last taboo – saying that you have a dreadful mother out loud – is something a lot of women are willing to talk, cry and laugh about.

After my second visit with K, a jailer told me that I could have interviewed every woman on the pod.

Who are these toxic moms?

They are moms who didn't hug, kiss, or say 'I love you.' Moms, who lied, cheated and stole. So many mothers, who looked nice in public, but pinched, slapped and belittled in private. They are mystery moms, intoxicated moms, and emotional "mom bombs."

❧ ❧

For the woman sitting in jail awaiting trial, her mom was the one who asked her 14-year-old daughter, "What's the big deal if a guy wants to go without a condom? More money for you."

During our conversations, we laughed a lot about her mom and horsed around with the subject of toxic mothers.

"How would you describe your mother's parenting style?" I asked her in mock seriousness holding my pencil high over my notepad.

She delivered her answer with a dramatic roll of her eyes.

"Bad."

She is just one woman willing to speak up about her toxic mom. She got nothing in return. I didn't write anything for the judge or the social workers. I'm not sure anyone would have let me anyway. I often think about this woman. She got out of jail and then I heard she was back in.

TOOLS

"For who will testify, who will accurately describe our lives if we do not do it ourselves?"
Faye Moskowitz, *And the Bridge is Love*

PEN & PAPER

No one is going to break into your home to look at what you write about your relationship with your toxic mother. So keep notes in a journal or on your laptop to help you track the highs and lows and recurring themes. Make notes on how what your mother says or does makes you feel. Data is good – especially if it helps you untangle the mystery of your toxic mother.

CHAPTER SIX

The Wooden Spoon Garden

MEMOIR

*M*y mother's tiny kitchen on 26th Avenue had black and white linoleum tiles with a huge double window over the sink. Our window looked directly into the neighbor's kitchen window across the dark alleyway.

When I was four, not yet old enough for school, I could put my big toe on the round knob to the cupboard below the sink and boost myself up, stretching my arm as long as it would reach to swing the metal faucet towards my pink lips.

By first grade, when I was seven, I could easily hop up with my rib cage over the sink's tile rim to slurp cold water. I could do it with my clattering metal roller skates on, even. It isn't until we are moving away from 26th Avenue when I'm eleven that I can finally drink with my feet on the floor.

The kitchen is where my mother makes bologna sandwiches for our lunches on a pullout breadboard. Always made the night before, she uses just one slice of pink Oscar Meyer bologna with mayonnaise and mustard on white bread. Always just a red apple. Always tossed in a brown paper bag. Just that. Nothing but bologna for the entire time we attended grammar school.

It's a summer morning because I'm wearing an old cotton dress; not ironed. The ties, which should make a nice bow behind my back, are hanging down brushing the tops of my faded navy blue tennies. My back is in the corner of the kitchen counters held in place by my mother's two fingers in my chest. The toaster squats on the counter above my head. My older brother is near me but keeps sliding along the one wall of drawers trying to inch his way towards the hall and the front door.

My father is not home.

My mother is upset.

She's in a fury about missing wooden spoons, accusing us of using them as toys, of burying them in the backyard, something that would never occur to either one of us.

My mother loved her wooden spoons. Nothing better for getting a child's attention. Her arm would swoop up and she would swing the whistling spoon down against the sides of our legs, over and over. Many times the spoon would break in half, making her even madder over the loss of a perfectly good spoon. I've been cracked in the back of the head with a wooden spoon. I've had my fanny and back of my legs bruised in tattoos made by the bowl of a wooden spoon.

Had I taken the broken pieces of all the destroyed spoons and buried them in our backyard what would have sprouted up in the spring? Would my wooden spoon garden be a scramble of thorns and brambles or would the most delicate and colorful flowers rise up and face the sun?

With one hand clutching my brother's shirtsleeve my mother rifled through a huge utensil drawer feeling for a smooth wood handle. As she stirred up a silver soup of gleaming cleavers, metal graters, a huge cake server, and expandable two pronged forks for barbecuing wieners, our terror rose.

I wore thick cat-eye glasses so my kid's cartoon logic whispered to me *she'd never get my eyes with those expando forks.*

We tried not to say a word or make a sound, because my mother in search of a wooden spoon we could live with. She'd broken so many of them on our legs, it seemed like a family tradition to uphold. My brother's sliding made her madder and madder until she slammed him back into place up against me.

In a little singsong voice she reminds us of a scene in a Tarzan movie we all saw on TV recently. I know what she intends immediately. We both do.

A row of African porters in loincloths suspected of stealing something are told by the Witch Doctor that liars can't keep saliva in their mouths under questioning. He holds a knife over a fire until it is red-hot. The natives telling the truth will have just enough spit to keep the knife from burning them. The Witch Doctor re-heats the knife, as he makes his way down the line of men. Each honest man only feels a sizzle of spit evaporating under the knife held flat on the tongue. Finally, the lying, thieving native is revealed with a blood curdling scream and a hiss of burning flesh.

My mother says maybe she should heat up a knife to see which one of us is lying, although neither of us has lied as far as we know. All we do is whimper and plead for release. She tells us to stand still, to open our mouths and keep them open and we do.

I'd like to remember that my brother held my hand or stood in front of me protectively, but in our house it was every man for himself. My brother was a jolter, a quick dasher, despite his asthma. My best defense was squirming. I could render my body as impossible to pick up as jelly dropped on a linoleum floor. I could wiggle like an oiled fish so long that any adult would give up from sheer frustration of trying to find something to latch onto.

My mother put two cubes of sugar and two small glasses of water on the sink counter, explaining that she will know which of us have lied by who grabs for something first. She then sprinkled Tabasco sauce from the funny shaped bottle into our mouths.

My brother grabs for the water, gulps it and manages to whiz by our mother at a gallop, slamming the front door behind him. I grab a sugar cube, figuring whether we are liars or not I'd rather have candy. I turn my back to her, my nose against the wall. I'm afraid she'll hurt my face. She regularly "flips" my lips with her glossy Jordan Almond nails.

I become hysterical over the burning that will not stop and I slide down onto the floor crying. My mother stands at the sink running water. I'm crying so hard snot is dropping on my dress on top of little Tabasco sauce flecks.

My mother looks over her shoulder smirking at me because she has determined which of her children lies. She lifts our biggest pot out of the sink, turns and dumps out gallons of cold water on me. She steps over me and out of the room saying over her shoulder, "Poor, Sarah Heartburn! Have a good cry Sarah! Life is so tough for you!"

What happened next? I can't remember. I could imagine tiptoeing out the backdoor and sitting on the porch in the sun to dry off. I might have told my troubles to our standard poodle, Monique.

Like a lot of kids growing up in San Francisco in the early sixties, our only rule was to come home when the streetlights came on. So, I was certainly free to go. My mother wouldn't miss me. She had naps to take. Make-up to apply. Phone calls to make.

Maybe I went next door where my friend's mother loaned me dry clothes and combed and braided my hair? No, I never asked anybody for help so nobody ever did that for me.

I most likely searched out my brother who was always leading a gang of kids in a game of Heats (hide-and-go-seek in teams), or digging a hole, building a fort or exploring Golden Gate Park, half a block away. We could have ridden our bikes over to the playground on 28th to see who was there playing, and if anyone wanted to see who could swing the highest or which one of us was willing to jump off the monkey bars.

There was the B&B Pharmacy two blocks away, where my brother daily folded 200 newspapers for his morning delivery route. The pharmacist let you read comic books in the store that smelled of aspirin and hair pomade as long as you were quiet and didn't block the aisles for real shoppers.

If anyone had more than a nickel, there was Charlie's candy store run by the husband and wife who both looked like grizzled old war veterans. We'd walk over to the top of the Balboa Hill overlooking our block and sit on the curb unwrapping, licking, and trading candy; dropping wrappers in the gutter grate, making ourselves sick until something else to do struck our fancy.

Construction sites were good hangouts for us because men swore and you might learn some new dirty words. Fire stations. No libraries where busybody women might ask us questions. Bus stops were fun. Anywhere with working men or men in uniforms. We once happily spent all day watching a construction crew hoisting an enormous gold onion dome onto the Russian Orthodox Church down on Geary Street.

As the sun set, one by one all the other kids got called into dinner. One mom with an Italian accent used to fling open a front window to yell, "An-TONE-eeeeeeeee. Time-a to come ome!" We were usually the last on the street, tinkering on our bikes or just hanging out on the front steps. Eventually, our dad would drive up in his rusted out Chevy and it would be safe to go back in again.

With our father's mere presence protecting us my mother resumed her homemaking activities. The Tabasco was hidden in the back of a dark shelf. The water had been sopped up off the floor. Standing in the kitchen frying up red potatoes she looked like any other mom using the wooden spoon to keep the potato skins from sticking to her sizzling cast iron pan.

"Good communication is as stimulating as black coffee and just as hard to sleep after."
Anne Morrow Lindbergh, *Gift from the Sea*

COFFEE DATES

Even if you don't want to or need to talk about your Toxic Mom schedule coffee dates with people who inspire you to be yourself. The more we connect with others, the less disconnected we feel.

CHAPTER SEVEN
Your Mother Might Be Toxic If...

 How bad was my mother? I have to rank her in the pantheon of toxic moms somewhere between Faye Dunaway in "Mommy Dearest" and Norma Bates in "Psycho." You remember Norma — the lady who wouldn't hurt a fly?

Which might make you wonder how toxic is your mom?

She might have dressed you funny or refused to let you go to sleep-away camp, but was she *really* so bad? To be fair, you could factor in times when money was tight or her cat died and cut her some retro-active slack. Considering her period of substance abuse, a divorce or mental illness back then could open the door to forgiveness.

Take a deep breath and look at my unscientific test to help you decide if your mother is truly toxic.

One point for every time you say to yourself, *oh yeah*.

YOUR MOTHER MAY BE TOXIC IF:

yes/no   When you see her number on caller I.D., you freeze.

yes/no   When it takes more than 15 minutes to warn new friends about how to act around her and teach them the silent signal for, *We're leaving!*

yes/no   You are certain that she views you as social or sexual competition.

yes/no   You really don't know very much about her life story or extended family.

yes/no   She lies about her age.

yes/no   She lies about *your* age.

yes/no   If you've lost track of more than five "uncles."

yes/no   Gifts from her regularly include silent messages of the need for improvement.

yes/no   She is quick to cut off family members who cross her.

yes/no   She keeps no photos from a significant portion of her life.

yes/no   She always has a faraway look or smirk on her face in family photos.

yes/no   She compulsively measures and monitors household supplies.

yes/no   Movies or commercials with strong mother/daughter themes get you weepy.

yes/no   You feel your mother loves you only when you are successful.

yes/no   You dread Mother's Day, celebrating her birthday or your own birthday.

yes/no   You feel anxious in the days leading up to family gatherings.

yes/no   Your mother was or is addicted to alcohol, drugs, sex, gambling or other destructive activities.

yes/no   She enjoys pitting one family member against another.

yes/no   She left you in the care of an irresponsible adult or an immature sibling, or left you home alone for extended periods of time.

yes/no   She gave you luggage for your high school graduation.

Usually these lists have a ranking at the end, but I'm going to leave that to you. Is ten "yeses" okay? Is one too much? That's entirely up to you. I left out several that apply only to me, like: If you were ever kidnapped and your mother didn't notice.

CHAPTER EIGHT
The Queen Of The Washington Club Bar

VOICES

"At one time she was the Queen of the Washington Club Bar. We'd go there to ask for lunch money and the bartender would give us free sodas."
- G, born 1961

She's been at a very low-paying job for years but she hangs in there convinced that God has more in store for her. She was a teen mother, a drug addict and dealer until she cleaned up over 15 years ago. She regularly speaks at Alcoholics Anonymous 12-step meetings and is a clean and sober mentor to several women in her community with similar backgrounds.

Nearly all her life, she's been trying to make peace with her mother.

"My mother was very pretty but when she drank, I was scared of her. She always would end up hitting us," she said.

Her mother had a beauty problem. She was the beauty of the Washington Club bar until she developed the ugly habit of falling off her stool. In her prime she was alluring enough to have married five times.

She was such a fixture in her favorite smoky watering hole that her children felt comfortable looking for her there on the way to and from school. When in the care of other relatives G and her sister would wave to the bar if they drove by. That's where their mother lived.

"When we got older we'd come in and have drinks with her. She always wanted to party, but with her it was never really a party," she said.

Her mom was the cool mom with a sad twist. She enjoyed drinking with her children and their friends. She was fine with boys staying overnight.

"She would buy us alcohol, drugs. She gave us money for cigarettes."

She'd come home from bars, sometimes with strange men, other times incoherent, mumbling and angry. She'd blast open her kids bedroom door, yelling. They quickly learned to fight back. Fight or their mother would hit them until her arms got tired.

"My mother was a whack-a-doo. When we were little, she'd come into our bedroom in the middle of the night and pull us out of bed by the hair. Even at 2 a.m. the fight would be ON!"

Growing up, G remembers feeling angry most of the time. When her mother brought home men, she would always have a crying fit.

"If I saw my mom kissing some man I'd break everything in my room including the window. I was so angry. I know now that what I wanted was her attention."

She attended Catholic schools from kindergarten until tenth grade when pregnancy forced her to transfer into a continuation school where she graduated only three months behind her original senior class.

At 16 she married an older man, not the father of her child. He was abusive.

Her solution was to get a job at an engraving shop for $1.75 an hour while her grandmother cared for her daughter. It was there that a fellow employee turned her onto PCP, speed, reds; whatever was available.

"We drank liquor at work fixing watches. And we'd be high. Eventually, I started using crank," she said.

Right when drug abuse caused her to spend more money than she made she also survived a serious car accident. Her bright idea was to go into business for herself.

"I dealt street drugs from my bedroom for the next seven years. It took a while for me to hit bottom."

She was putting tremendous energy into suing someone over a wreck she caused. The lawyer handling her car accident case realized that she had severe drug issues and suggested she seek help. He said she should talk to a therapist.

"I was blaming everyone but myself when I ran into them and was totally on drugs. I will always remember the psychiatrist telling me I use this giggling humor thing to make myself feel better."

Yes, she jokes about her mother.

"My friends at work are like *'Oh my God!'* when I say bad things about her. But I've done a lot of work to forgive my mother and I'm usually laughing when I'm telling stories about her."

With therapy she figured out a lot about her mother and the family history. Her mother's mother was a hard working nurse and the savoir to many dysfunctional members of her brood. This grandmother had been raped as a young girl and married her rapist, a second cousin.

"She was a worker. Work, work, work. Always saving. Never spending. That's how she could afford to bail us out all the time."

She also covered up everything her children and extended family had problems with. One son died in a wretched state due to alcoholism. It just wasn't discussed.

"I once told her bailing me out (of jail) kept me in trouble because it never really got so bad. She was mad. She called me ungrateful."

The grandmother also spent many years saving her daughter, the Queen of the Washington Bar, from attempt after attempt at suicide. There were so many incidents, so many threats that G became hardened to her mother's histrionics.

"It got to the point when the phone call would come from my grandmother I'd say, I'm not rushing to any hospital. I'll get there when I get there. I'm doing my nails."

And yet the mother and daughter did not have long periods of estrangement. They might take a break of a few weeks from each other, but they always spoke by phone. They stayed connected.

"She used to say she was an alcoholic but I was a drug addict. 'What you do is illegal,' she'd tell me and I'd say, yeah, but I know my name all day."

When G was deep into drugs, her mother would always offer to let her sleep in her little trailer.

"She'd say just come home. And I'd say *home?* That's not my home."

"When I got clean, I thought that I would get her to go to meetings with me. Every morning I'd call her and every morning she'd have an excuse. She'd tell me a story. *I felt sick and I took cold medicine so I can't go.* I really tried with all my heart to sober her up."

G had a fantasy about a new, clean mother/daughter relationship. Meetings were the trick. Coffee and talk would be her mother's magic bullet. They would get clean together and then they'd speak at meetings together. They'd be a mother/daughter sobriety act.

"Of course in telling others how bad it was I'd make her suffer. I'd make her tell it over and over. Throw it in her face a little," she said laughing.

But her mother died within a year of her daughter's sobriety.

"When I was out there, I did what I did. I can't undo anything. I pretty much did what my mother did to us. My mother was the life of the party. The party was more important than us.

I've done a lot of work to forgive my mother for what she did. I realize that I also made my kids feel not important. They knew me and drugs were more important. But my kids didn't have to step over strange men on the floor. I didn't drink or party with my kids. I didn't lose my kids."

"Only you can forgive you. I had to forgive myself to forgive my mother."

At family gatherings G is often compared to her mother for her laughter and zest for life.

"I'm okay with that. What they are really saying is that we are both fun. She was pretty and fun, and there were times when I was in heaven over having such a cool mom. Now, I'd kick that mom's ass."

G keeps a nicely framed photo of her mother as a hot looking teenager on the family room wall.

"The other day I looked at it and said, 'I really need you right now. Why did you have to be like that?'"

TOOLS

**"Your vision will become clear only
when you can look into your own
heart. Who looks outside, dreams;
who looks inside, awakens."**

– Carl Jung

SANE FRAMES

When your toxic mother is overly demanding, guilt-inducing or emotionally blackmailing, put on your imaginary Sane Eyeglasses and ask yourself: If any person other than my mother did this would I take it? You may have perfect vision but keep your Sane Eyeglasses handy for emotional emergencies.

CHAPTER NINE

Ask Yourself: 20 Crucial Questions for Daughters of Toxic Mothers

TOXIC MOM TOOLKIT
SELF-TEST

1. Can you describe your relationship with your mother when you were a child, a teen and when you were a young adult?

2. Have you seen your own birth certificate? If not, why not?

3. Have you seen your mother's birth certificate and her marriage license(s)? If not, why not? (They are public records.)

4. Fill in the blanks to the following paragraph. If you cannot, why can't you?

   My mother was born in 19____ in _____, _____(city/state/country) to parents _____(father) and _____ (mother). She was the _____(first, second, etc.) daughter among _____ siblings of _____ girls and

_____ boys. She lived in _____(a house, an apartment or farm) until the _____ grade. By
the time she was 18 she was _____(accepted
to college, began work, was married, etc.). The biggest
trauma of her life was _____. Her biggest
accomplishment in life has been _____.

5. What do you know about your mother's life before you were
   conceived?

6. How did (does) your mother get along with her own mother?

7. How old were you when you first realized that your mother
   was different than other mothers? In what ways?

8. When you have been ready to defend yourself to your mother – to speak up or speak back – how has she silenced you?
   Have you silenced yourself? Why?

9. Did your mother ever have substance abuse issues such as
   alcohol, drug use or inappropriate or risky sexual behaviors?
   Did she have periods of mental illness or mental instability?
   If so, for what periods of your life?

10. How many times during your childhood did you move? Do
    you know why your family moved?

11. Was there any family tragedy or need to focus on another sibling that may have negatively affected your relationship with your mother?

12. If you were neglected, verbally or sexually abused, or otherwise mistreated did you seek help? Should you consider seeking therapeutic help today? If not, why not?

13. During significant periods of estrangement how easy or difficult was it to limit or cut off contact with your mother?

14. How has your relationship with your mother affected your relationships with other members of your immediate family? How has it affected friendships, getting along with co-workers, or being part of your chosen communities?

15. To whom can you speak honestly about your toxic mother?

16. Given your current levels of contact with your mother how are you viewed within your family? How does that feel?

17. Can you list three wonderful things your mother has done for you? Giving birth or throwing a wedding doesn't count.

18. What is your biggest criticism of your mother? Are your criticisms valid?

19. What would she criticize about you? Are her criticisms valid?

20. As your mother ages, do you see yourself having more or less contact with her? Why?

CHAPTER TEN
Mission: Britex Fabrics

MEMOIR

*A*bout half way through writing this book, on the spur of the moment I drove down to San Francisco from the wine country. It was a rare day on which I could make up my own schedule. I felt relaxed and I was smiling at other drivers. I had a sudden urge to go to Britex Fabrics, the last outpost of quality yardage in the universe.

I had forgotten how it felt to just know a town like the back of your hand, to easily wheel by the stations of your life. It was an overdue break in my routine, an escape from the retina-scalding laptop and writing.

I parked at my favorite garage near Union Square and tripped down Stockton to Maiden Lane, where, when I was a little girl, each Wednesday with an early pass from school, I went to my eye exercises at Dr. LeBlanc's, whose elderly wife was also his nurse. The doctor was white haired and they both wore white uniforms and smelled of cleansing chemicals.

I was born severely cross-eyed. When I began school in the early 1960's the most common method for correction was alternating patches over my eyes. I was that kid with the dirty flesh-colored Band-Aid over one eye for a week and then the other was covered the next week. I always had gummy latex traces where the edge of the bandage used to be. The method worked, but very slowly.

It was decided that a special eye doctor could help speed the process. Utilizing a method where the patient enters a dark room, sits with their chin resting on a huge mechanical apparatus with dual screens, one for each eye, focusing on dual images of very busy slide photographs like European cathedrals. At five or ten minute intervals the nurse would calibrate the screens to move slightly apart, thus training the eyes to pull more evenly towards a center for optimal vision. For a child it was agony and actually rather tiring and I was always promised a treat afterwards.

At first my mother took me, but for some reason my grandmother (my dad's mother) took over the duty. She would arrive at my grammar school with a perfect little half tuna sandwich neatly wrapped in waxed paper, which I would eat on the drive downtown washed down by a tiny carton of chocolate milk.

After completing an hour of eye exercises, my grandmother and I would make our window-shopping rounds. We'd walk to Britex Fabrics and up the creaking carpeted staircases to the notions floor to buy ribbon or snaps or new glittery buttons for her old bronze-colored housecoat.

Next stop: Robison's Pets. It's the pet shop immortalized by Alfred Hitchcock in the opening scene of "The Birds." They had a wall of ornate white cages behind a thin chain hung like a velvet rope at a nightclub. The staff would let you test drive kittens, or play peek-a-boo with puppies.

Upstairs at Robison's were oodles of birds in floor to ceiling roosts. They had everything from jungle parrots that would outlive you to finches the size of your thumb. For a child it was pet-smell wood chip heaven. When I was older, they stocked the rhinestone collars punk rockers bought for club necklaces and bracelets.

After Robison's we might head over to Blum's bakery for toffee cake. I needed help climbing up to sit on stools that could spin while I waited for our plates to slide along a shiny counter towards us. Sometimes we found ourselves at the TWA office (an all glass Mad Men corner storefront) to buy a teeny-tiny zippered flight bag filled with salt-water taffy.

We wrapped up our afternoon downtown at our favorite watering hole, The Top of the Mark. I don't remember what my grandmother ordered, although it was definitely a stiff drink, but I always ordered a Shirley Temple with maraschino cherries because it came with a plastic monkey riding the lip of the hi-ball glass. I knew it would never happen, but as the bartender worked with his back towards us I dreamed of snagging the much more rare and substantially larger orange plastic giraffe drink stir sticks I'd found so many times at the bottom of my mother's pocketbook.

My grandmother was almost too fancy to be a grandmother.

Driving around San Francisco, I couldn't get my grandmother out of my head. It was my grandmother who introduced me to the ladies room at I. Magnin's. The make-up area had a long counter, and low-slung chairs and gleaming mirrors. Beyond that was a big square room slathered in thick white marble with only three sinks spaced along the far wall. It might take a newcomer a beat to notice the "occupied" "not occupied" cylinders imbedded along the opposite wall. The doors to the actual toilets were put in so precisely, the seams of marble so tight, that it was almost an optical illusion of a solid wall.

Once you stepped into a toilet station clicking the door behind you it was as silent as a tomb in the stall.

"The lovely thing about I. Magnin's is you can shop all day and then go into a stall and scream your head off," my grandmother told me.

One day when I was very little, I was home alone playing on one of the three green shag throw rugs scattered in our den. I was cutting thick paper with gleaming scissors, making little boxes with lids. I never cared for dolls. But give me some good construction paper, scissors and tape and I was a happy kiddy carton manufacturer.

I looked up and there was my grandmother, her shiny alligator pocketbook hanging from her wrist. She was so beautiful - always dressed up with every blonde curl in place, her fox furs smelling of exotic perfume.

She asked me where my mother was.

I said I didn't know.

It was a weekday and I was home earlier than my older brother who must have still been at school. My grandmother asked if I'd like to go to the zoo. We both knew they fed the lions at 2 p.m.

Wouldn't that be fun?

I don't remember much about that day other than it was a nice treat to see my grandmother and that it was fun to leave the house. We went to Golden Gate Park by the museum, the old deYoung with the fishpond in front. I rubbed the noses of the pair of gigantic terra cotta lions set above the people traversing the path along the road in front of the museum.

And then we were back at the flat and the mood was black.

Where had we been my mother wanted to know and my grandmother wanted to know the same of my mother. *That was none of my grandmother's business,* my mother said. My mother said she could call the police. *You can't just take children for the day.*

You can if no one is watching the baby and you are the grandmother, my grandmother said.

Then it blurs.

❧ ❧

When they were newlyweds, my parents lived with my dad's parents on Cole and Clayton streets in the Haight. So I have to believe my grandmother knew what she knew.

I can't remember the last time I thought about my grandmother for a second, let alone the better part of a day. It was like my grandmother was in the car with me, and standing next to me at the Britex counter buying ribbon.

I was having a sentimental journey including flashbacks from Playland at the Beach; holiday roof rides at The Emporium department store, and so many of my grandmother's fleeting appearances in my young life.

Then it hit me. My grandmother tried to stick up for me.

Who knows where my mother was the day my grandmother kidnapped me. Even if she had picked me up from preschool my mother left a five- or six-year-old alone from noon to at least two. I have to think she figured my brother would be home after his school, which let out at 3:10 p.m. She could have been drinking, out with a man, or just playing tennis. She felt leaving me at home with scissors and paper was perfectly fine. She had probably done it many times.

A trip to the City, my hometown, to the streets that were always wet with fog and riddled with snail tracks reminded me of the curious case of Baby Rayne's kidnapping by her own grandmother.

That's when it hit me that sentimental journeys are part of dreams – or should be. When you finally knuckle down and focus on that goal you take all your experiences with you. That's why you have to befriend your experiences, good or bad. They comprise your story and make you who you are. The bad parts can't hurt you without your permission. The good parts make you think.

I had plenty of gas, so I rolled through Golden Gate Park, past the tennis courts where my married mother met many of her beaus. I drove by the newly constructed starkly designed ultra modern DeYoung Museum. I swung down Geary Boulevard nearly missing a squirrelly cyclist darting in and out of traffic. When I saw a parking space right in front of Bill's on Clement Street I stopped in for a *turkey platter* of French fries and a Coke.

Afterwards, I walked over to the old Wirth's Bros. bakery on 23rd Avenue, now a Chinese bakery with mostly Russian customers, to buy a perfectly awful sugar cookie shaped like a rooster with the best hard icing that crackled when I bit it.

When we lived on 26th Avenue my brother used to put me on his bike handlebars and we'd ride over to Wirth's buy a Danish wreath for breakfast. I remembered it from a kid's perspective: my eyes level to the doorknob of that wonderful glass door. Inside the vanilla perfumed bakery holding our dollar bills up as high as we could for the lady at the cash register.

I walked past blocks of buildings whose windows have watched me grow up. I cruised by the Russian church and remembered the day I sat on the curb watching them lift the glittering domes from a flatbed truck.

It was a sentimental journey, reminding me of the sights and smells, the brass doorknobs rubbed gold and the occasional two- by three-inch speakeasy peepholes carved into the fourth step of so many old lobby stairways.

It was like the streets and buildings and windows and doors were looking back at me. *Look, she's all grown up and she's okay. We knew she'd turn out okay.*

Someone in my family did see what was happening and did try in her own way to intervene. It couldn't have been much fun to show your son that his wife was untrustworthy.

I drove back home re-crossing the Golden Gate Bridge still smiling at the other drivers.

CHAPTER ELEVEN

The Good Kind Of Spousal Support

VOICES

"I would like to have a good relationship with my mom but in my heart I know that there will always be drama with her."

- J, born 1977

Her parents were both alcoholics who fought constantly through three marriages to and two divorces from each other.

"Growing up they always fought, so my home was always in disarray. Maybe in those early days they were in love. But all I remember is my mom always being a smart ass to my dad and nagging him over everything," said J.

J's mother grew up in the East and her family moved to California when she was ten years old. Her younger brother was nine years younger and was doted on as the baby of the family. By the time J's mother graduated from high school her parents divorced and her mother became a party girl, staying out late at night trying to have a good time.

J's mother met a man and became pregnant at 19. It was around the time of her pregnancy that J's mom noticed that her mother's youngest son was left alone at night. He was getting into drugs and alcohol so she tried to help her younger brother. Eventually, he moved to Hawaii, mainly to get away from his mother. He died of an overdose when he was 32.

"My grandma then spent all of her time at his grave, I think six to seven days a week and her life was never the same," J said.

Because her first husband physically abused her, when her son was just six months old J's mother moved back in with her own mother. She met her second husband in a bar. They eventually married three times and divorced twice. They are still married.

"He had a construction business and was making good money. I think my mom never fell in love with him but saw him as a way out of her problems."

J's parents divorced first when she was five years old and remarried the first time when she was seven or eight.

"I believe that my dad truly loved my mom and arguing was his way of trying to reason with her. But over the years he just gave up and he has no more fight left. That's what my mom does to people close to her. She wears them down and tears them apart."

Her parents are able to go grocery shopping together and enjoy dining out, but J's father has a system for living at home. He has a small office with a television and he ducks in there to watch shows alone. He is a man in a permanent retreat in his own home.

J remembers a happy childhood in general, but can't remember her mother interacting with her much. As soon as J began wanting to do normal teen activities – talking on the phone, hanging out with friends – her mother started verbally riding her. She could go, but J knew that when she came home she would have to be excoriated verbally by her mother. She would be torn down, picked apart.

By 19, J had been working and making a little money as a cosmetologist. An extraordinarily pretty girl, she was made to feel ugly and "not enough," which led to a bout with bulimic eating.

"I became bulimic because I couldn't handle the stress. It was my way of owning my control over myself."

She moved back home when she was 20. At that time she was working full time in an office.

"If I wanted to go to the gym after work or hang out with friends I had to call my mother who would fly off the handle. She wanted me home for dinner because she cooked 'a nice dinner.' I would hang up and within minutes my father would call me back to give me more grief about not coming home on time."

She remembers her mother embarrassing her in restaurants at this time. Her mother would complain loudly that she didn't want to spend good money if J was just going to throw it all up.

She moved two hours away. When J was 22 she found a therapist who helped her see that she was not bad, not crazy for reacting the way she did to her own mother. The bulimia faded. Eventually she married and had two children. She credits her husband's amazing support with helping her develop the perspective she needed in order to see that her mother's behavior was more than just annoying, but actually destructive, toxic.

Like a lot of young couples, when J and her husband started off they experienced financial challenges. J's mother was Johnny-on-the-spot with loans and groceries. That way she had leverage to demand 24/7 access to her daughter's home and excessive amounts of time with her grandchildren.

"My mother would call several times a day, driving me crazy. She thought because I was a stay-at-home mother that meant she could drop in whenever she liked. If I asked her not to come over it became a fight."

It was draining.

"My mother can easily say things and make you question yourself. She can make you feel so guilty and insecure. Her words cut like a knife. She is just always there... demanding full attention. Whatever I want to do is not right, or won't work out. She can take anything positive and turn it into a negative."

She feels her relationship with her mother has caused her to lose friends.

"If I talked about it, they just didn't understand where I was coming from because they had normal moms. Maybe I talked about it too much? I've now learned not to say anything about my mother to new people."

Her mother continues to call relentlessly. When the phone rings J cringes but answers. She would like to set boundaries. Her husband says she doesn't have to pick up the phone. He says unplug the phone, but J can't.

She went online for answers and found Toxic Mom Toolkit. She became one of the earliest visitors offering support to others looking for answers. She is still working on setting boundaries. She knows that she's not a bad person but feels like one whenever she says "no" to her mother.

"I would like to have a good relationship with my mom but in my heart I know that there will always be drama with her. I am a mother and a wife, not just her daughter. So I guess I would like to have less contact with her because the more communication I have with her the more toxic my life becomes."

TOOL

"They always say time changes things, but you actually have to change them yourself."
– Andy Warhol

EGG TIMER

Keep a timer on or near your phone and decide ahead how much time you allot to your mother. If she gets ten minutes and the buzzer sounds say your goodbyes and hang up. You can allot different times for different days of the week or holidays, but maintain control of the time spent on the phone with your Toxic Mom.

CHAPTER 12

The Cat's Paw Kid

MEMOIR

*W*hen my brother was 14-years old and I was nine, we lived through an unusually hot summer for San Francisco. It was the summer our parents' marriage was cracking up, when windows left open at night allowed rivers of dirty arguments between them to flow through our neighborhood.

Cascading bath water masked my father's crying. Doors slammed. Cars started up in the dead of night in the garage below our bedrooms.

My father called Chicken Delight a lot.

"Don't cook tonight - call Chicken Delight!" went the television jingle. We gorged on super-crunchy fried chicken deliveries that arrived piping hot inside two yellow paper plates stapled together. We were happy to get flying saucer chicken spaceships for dinner. We called in orders so often, the number was written in pencil on the kitchen doorjamb.

That summer other mothers on the block took special care of us inviting us for dinners, bandaging our scrapes, including us in their kids' plans. We were allowed our roaming and comforted instead of scolded when we went too far.

Because my parents often "parked" us at the movies all day most weekends, we had recently seen a couple of gangster movies about Prohibition Chicago and greatly admired the crime planning scenes. We liked the way they called robbery plans "jobs." So we started planning our own jobs. Like giving our poodle our vegetables. That job went off without a hitch. Then came the ringing doorbells and running jobs. Those were night capers – fewer witnesses. A nearly daily job involved turning off apartment building elevators. An inside job since my brother – the News Call newspaper delivery boy – had keys to every building in our neighborhood.

Come to think of it, that summer was full of our odd kiddy crimes. There was the teensy-weenie fire my brother and I accidentally started in the basement storage room under our own flat where our neighbor stored boxes of sugar packets. I was a kid with a 'what if' mind. I wanted to know if sugar would burn. It wouldn't have been so bad if we hadn't also recently removed and lost the small metal handle of the garage hose. My dad, who had one hand with fingers cut off due to a print shop accident, had to pinch the little water valve stem and turn with all his might to get a dribble from the hose and douse the blaze.

There was the day I encouraged my brother to drop a rock on the neighbor boy's head as he crawled low like the soldiers on "Combat!"

along the other side of our fence. No one can say I wasn't persuasive. You should have seen the blood.

I was a great crime organizer. I had a gang that threw snails and dirt clods at our neighbor's fresh laundry hanging on the backyard clothesline. That spree went on for weeks driving the poor woman to tears. As I recall, she was a Holocaust survivor. When we tired of ruining her laundry we took to smashing her egg and milk deliveries. My dad had to pay for that.

We stole pocket money, lied, and stayed out late, and "forgot" to tell our parents when we slept over at friends.

Maybe our folks were glad to get us out of the house.

Before that summer, we had always been allowed to leave the connecting door between our two bedrooms open each night just long enough to talk quietly for a few minutes, like inmates before lights out and the clang of the locks being thrown. I'd ask my brother to sing the song from Rawhide, or I'd ask questions about why salt melts snails. Eventually my mother would come back in and close the door with a solid click signifying the true end of the day.

We were surprised when our door was left wide open all night every night and nobody bothered to shut it anymore. We would whisper in the dark at our end of the flat while our parent's volleyed insults in the living room.

"What if dad took you and mom took me?" I'd ask my brother.

"Will we still go to Russian River for summer?"

"Where will our dog go?"

My brother would cut short my worries by offering up something we could sing together – a jingle from a TV show like the Flintstones or the Huckleberry Hound song, or a new 45 record.

Honey Comb, won't you be my baby? Oh, Honey Comb, be my own.

Between delivering the morning newspaper and working for the B&B Pharmacy on weekends, my brother was always running in squeaky Converse sneakers. He always dashed off, shunning my company. He could be driven mad by my little sister peskiness, and on many occasions, tied me up with his soft bathrobe belt leaving me in his dirty clothes hamper. There I would lie quietly like Moses in the rushes until my mother lifted the lid, scaring the bejeezus out of her.

To my surprise, my brother began allowing me to tag along on his trips around the neighborhood. He quit holding me by the wrist like a baby and only held the back of my neck while crossing the street.

Looking back, I know now that we were sticking together just trying to make sense of everything. Our parents, who never had secrets before, were now very secretive. Naturally, secret things and places soon held the most fascination for us. We began haunting neighborhood basements and creepy boiler rooms imagining hidden rooms existed for us to find.

We spent hours exploring paths and shortcuts in Golden Gate Park. We began to go through our parent's drawers and closets whenever they were out. We dog-eared our adoption papers, their marriage certificate and vaccination records praying our parents wouldn't notice.

We spent that summer haunting our own neighborhood. My brother would wake me up in the dead of night and we would shimmy down the drainpipe outside my bedroom window, land on a low wood fence and jump into the neighbors grass. We walked through pitch black alleyways and up and down creaking back staircases, searching, searching, always looking for I don't know what.

We called these nocturnal meanderings our "jobs." We always left our mark. We rearranged potted plants; moved garbage cans from alleyways to just outside some widow lady's back door. We switched every other tenant's doormats along long apartment building corridors. We would stand on apartment building roofs and throw tar gravel or empty Coke cans on passing Muni buses and then run whooping like Indians, pounding down the stairs, melting into the labyrinth of backyards we knew so well. We threw things off rooftops like it was our job. Like we carried lunch pails and punched time cards like Sam the sheepdog and Ralph the wolf, in cartoons.

On the few occasions we were caught dead to rights by other adults, my father was in charge of punishing us in my brother's room. After pushing my mother from the scene and punching in the button on the doorknob to lock the door, my father would pull his thick belt out of the loops. The one with the great big buckle. It landed on the mattress with a tremendous smack as we hid our faces in the corner and cried out in a syncopated beat. My mother stood on the other side of the door, admonishing my dad, saying *maybe that's enough* not realizing that he was only showing us how strong his whipping arm was – should he ever choose to punish us corporally. The faux spanking drama would slow us down making us contrite for a day or two. It was too hard on our dad.

Yet, our jobs continued.

With a new school year on the horizon we planned our final summer caper, a 3 a.m. walkthrough of our neighbor's flat. They were our parent's best friends, and we were allowed to call them by their first names, and we thought of them as our aunt and uncle. Their kids were our best friends. We spent as much time in their home as we did in our own. They had the identical floor plan, only flipped.

My brother woke me up and helped me put on my lace-less, stinky, blue Keds. We tiptoed down the hall to our little half bathroom, locking the door behind us. My brother climbed out our window into the light well and, standing on a horizontal pipe one story up, pulled me out easily.

It was a windless Indian summer night when people sprinkled water on their bed sheets out of fitful desperation to keep cool.

We planned to climb from the first story to the second story. My brother told me not to look down. As I looked way up at the miniature window on the other side of the airshaft, a breeze rippled across my sunburned arms giving me goose pimples. I was the cat's paw, the little criminal that got into small spaces then reached around and let the rest of the gang in. I'd go through the tiny two-foot by one-foot window, without knocking anything over on the inside, then tiptoe down a flight of stairs to let my brother in through the neighbor's front door.

We climbed up the big pipes running along the wall of the buildings. My brother moved loosely, confidently, like a tree jumping monkey. I moved more like a starfish inching its way across rocks in a crashing surf, stopping several times to gather the courage to keep going. I pressed my face against the cold pig-iron pipes for reassurance. Before long he opened the window then pushed me through it.

Inside I slid silently over the toilet, traversed the bathroom, slipped down the hall and went down a long, steep set of carpeted stairs hoping they wouldn't creak too loudly. I had to wait for my brother, who was too big to fit through the tiny window, to go back in our house and come around. Together in the hallway we stood in the dark for a long time, our hearts pounding, waiting for our breathing to become softer, quieter. The job was to walk through every room in the house, even the bedrooms where the family slept, and then leave through the front door.

Leaving the front door wide open was our mark.

We walked down the hall towards the back of the flat side by side, carefully placing one foot in front of the other, blind eyes wide open and arms stretched out to graze the walls. Sounds of the sleeping family skittered past us like bats, catching in our hair, penetrating our grinning ears.

We stood at the foot of our neighborly aunt and uncle's green satin quilted king-sized bed like children up too early on Christmas morning. Their bedside clock radio illuminated them just enough to see that they slept closely, entwined, snug. Taking in the scene made us too demoralized to go on. My brother finally put his hand on the back of my neck and turned me toward the doorway to go.

With our final job of the summer completed, we stood out on the sidewalk in front of our house under a flickering streetlight while everyone else in the whole world was asleep. Tired from crime nerves, I still insisted we dared to walk back in our own front door, agonizing over the amplified clomp of our front door handle.

We easily crept past our dad asleep on the couch. The real risk was walking past our mother's locked bedroom door as she was known to throw it open and beg for quiet at the slightest shift in the air.

Miraculously, we achieved the home base of our own small beds, climbing into them in our play clothes, not caring if we were found out in the morning. I remember smiling as I fell to sleep snug in my dirty, rust smeared white sweatshirt. On the eve of everything changing for our family, at least I realized something important about myself. I was a brave girl.

CHAPTER 13

Public Affection, Private Criticism: Why some daughters of toxic mothers choose never to have children.

VOICES

"'What are you, stupid? Are you a moron?
An imbecile?' my mother would say, but
never in front of other people; never with
other ears around." – P, born 1954

P is the daughter of a toxic mother, a middle sister to two brothers who all grew up on the East Coast. She describes her family as middle class.

"No extras, nothing extravagant. Working parents, including my mother," she said.

But that's not exactly true. The one thing her mother had bushels full of was venom for a devoted daughter who she felt was stupid; a moron.

"I know my mother did the best she could with what she had but I think she was probably mentally unstable and it went undiagnosed for her whole life because she was so smart," P said. "I also believe she was abused by her own mother and perhaps it was a cycle that had gone on for generations."

She describes her mother's toxicity as emanating from her face.

"It was the way she looked at me when she said, or thought, something. It was a face of such disgust," she recalled.

"My mother's overall underlying criticism of me, I believed, was the ugly seed. That until recently, made me feel 'less than' in so many ways."

And yet, her mother was always quick to praise her in public. She would brag about her daughter's accomplishments in school and praise her for being a good daughter. But then she would flip in private excoriating her daughter for minor transgressions, scolding her for being a dumbbell on a minute-by-minute basis.

When P turned 14, her father, whom she loved very much, died. That's when the toxic treatment she received from her mother accelerated.

"As an adult I can wonder how she could say these things to a kid, let alone your own child… How confusing is it to a child who only looks at her mother with eyes of love, to hear those things and feel that disgust? I am sure many parents call their kids stupid but how many called them an 'ungrateful wretch' or a 'useless piece of humanity?' She acted like she adored me in public and I thought *If they only knew what was said behind closed doors."*

After her father was gone, P became her mother's hired help, the slave, and the innocent one who never answered back, who would never, ever talk back.

"Her praising me in public? That was fake. I see it as a way to keep me doing what she wanted and needed and not what I needed as a person or a daughter," she said.

As a teenager, when most girls experience a period of rebellion, she was her mothers "best friend."

"My mother leaned on me. I was not wise enough to know I was being used and abused emotionally. As time went on, all I did was put her needs first," she said.

Indeed, as her mother aged and eventually required a caretaker, it was P who was chosen. By then her mother had successfully poisoned all P's siblings against each other, further isolating her daughter.

P has sought therapy for issues arising from her mother's treatment. She holds an associate's degree in Early Childhood Education, a Bachelor's in Social Work, a master's degree in Criminal Justice, and a certificate in Marriage and Family Therapy.

She has known her mother was a bad mother her whole life, but it took her a long time to seek out support. At first, going to therapy didn't help. But she kept looking for a therapist that truly understood toxic mother-daughter relationships.

"A friend who had problems with her mother recommended this therapist who is a saint in understanding the big picture. She did not patronize me. She got it."

In 2009, P's mom was moved to an assisted living facility because of the onset of Alzheimer's disease. In 2010 the diagnosis was confirmed. It was the window of opportunity P needed to physically distance herself from her toxic mom.

"It was time for me to go after years of distancing myself from her in different ways. For instance, I would decide ahead of time how much time I could stay to visit, how many minutes she got on the phone," she said.

Since moving away, P has experienced numerous epiphanies about her mother and their relationship.

"I think I always saw it for what it was, but was unable to feel it in my heart and soul until very recently. I repressed and suppressed many feelings, which I am now allowing myself to feel and cry about in order to get through them and past them."

One of those epiphanies was about her own life without her own children.

A divorced woman in her fifties, P has no children although when she was younger she always thought she would. Studying her family history, she understands that her grandmother verbally abused her mother. She suspects that there is a generational cycle, one she would never want to perpetuate. Maybe that was in the back of her mind all along.

"If I had children, I would have to limit my mother's time with them because of how I thought she would influence them. I saw her repeat negative words and deeds with my nieces and nephews and am sure it would have happened with my family as well, had I had children."

Ironically, having no children, no anchors in the community where her mother is institutionalized because of progressive Alzheimer's, allowed P her freedom.

"I'm sure my brothers and sisters-in-law envy me for having the courage to leave... Now I have freedom and solitude and no regrets," she said. "I did everything for her for 99 percent of my life. I have a clean compassionate conscience."

A note from P:

When re-reading my 'confessions' of my toxic mom history, I realize how raw and honest I was in sharing it, even though it was just the tip of the iceberg. It was a little scary putting it out there.

Over a year has gone by since I wrote it. I recently decided to move back east -- putting me in closer proximity to the line of fire -- but the freedom I experienced in the southwest has given me the clarity I need to be stronger, with boundaries much more defined. Oddly enough, I have more compassion for my mother but less for my brothers, who seem to have distanced themselves even further from me, again, the result of what I believe to be the continued demise of our fractured family and my mother's underlying, over-the-years, critical wrath. Thankfully, I am returning to the continued, unwavering support of many friends, who are my chosen family.

As for my mother, I wobble between pity, tolerance and sadness for her, while I march forward with my own life, erasing the tapes in my head of things she said so long ago. I keep myself happy by my faith, by keeping busy, being semi retired, semi self employed, by being with friends, by volunteering, and by hanging out with dogs -- the four legged kind -- they bring the most joy! For the record, I do love my mother and will miss her -- and the chances we never had -- when she goes. I know she did the best she could. I am honored to be part of this book and I thank Rayne for being brave enough to write it.

CHAPTER 14

Swinging Sixties Christmas

I grew up in the early sixties before The Beatles invaded, even before hippies tripped to Grace Slick at Bill Graham's Fillmore West.

At Christmastime, we posed for photos in front of flocked trees with bubbler lights and too much colored tinsel. And usually, because my family was small, we banded together with the other young families on the block and had some sort of holiday party during which one dad disappeared right before Santa Claus showed up with a wet, gooey, shaving cream beard.

We believed in Santa passionately and would argue with older kids when they tried to fill us in – or rather, ruin Christmas for us. Our parents were poor enough to carry paper bag lunches out the door each morning, but we always believed that wonderful things would await us Christmas morning.

By the time I was five or six my mother had managed to completely erase any family connections on her side. We were told we came from a very small family. In fact, as far as she was concerned, our family was just the four of us. And you buy that as a kid. It takes decades before you realize that it's a gyp. It takes a long time before you have that "A-ha!" moment and realize that your parent climbed up into the family tree long ago and sawed off all the strongest limbs. NOBODY comes from a small family. The human family is huge in interconnected until one person runs away from their own family and then lies to their children about it.

On my father's side there were my grandparents who, like a lot of people of their generation, didn't approve of adopting kids and my dad's twin brother, our uncle who had two sons, our cousins, who were each about our age. I can only remember one Christmas when a long table was set and the doorbell rang and friends and relatives came and went bearing gifts and good wishes. I must have been three or four.

For most of my childhood Christmas was my dad's department. He believed in tall trees, lots of lights and tinsel. He supplemented our main presents with as many 25-cent Chinatown presents he could find, wrap and stuff under the tree.

I look at old photos now and I can tell you which bin or shelf each toy came off of at our local Geary Boulevard dime store. The Lincoln Logs were by the front door. Airplane models were on the back wall. The cans of Pick-Up-Stix and decks of cards were closer to the cash register. We never got a puppy or a toy car or anything big and flamboyant, but we were kids and we enjoyed ripping off the colorful paper and lifting a small cloth doll or shiny harmonica out of its perfect box.

Our Christmas Eve tradition was pure sixties. My father, who never liked to wear, or do whatever the next guy did, crafted together a life-sized stuffed woman, named Mabel, using one of my grandmother's WWII-era suits with pointy shoulder pads, a pair of thick hose for legs, gloves for hands and a wig made from shiny brown unspun reel-to-reel recording tape.

We wanted Santa to come to our house first and stay so long he had to leave us other kids' presents. So, up would go Mabel on a comfy chair with one stuffed knee crossed over the other. On a TV tray nearby my dad would pour a shot of whiskey in a small tumbler and lay out a couple of cigarettes.

"Forget cookies and milk!" my dad would crow.

We thought this was normal.

I didn't think every kid had a Mabel to put out. But I supposed they had a Sally or Gracie. I had to be 25-years-old before the thought of my dad putting out Mabel made me laugh. Before then, I always thought Mabel was normal.

At our house, each year, as I carefully distribute decorations around the living room and balance the long evergreen swag atop the fireplace mantle, I make sure there is a little space for the only photograph I have of my dad and Mabel. It's a tiny black and white framed print showing my dad on one knee, gallantly kissing the cloth hand of Mabel.

If the house caught on fire, that's what I would run back in to save.

CHAPTER 15

Mother's Day Down Under

VOICES

"My mother has a habit of collecting every little thing I've ever done "wrong" and then mentioning these things going way, way back.
- F, born 1975

Mother's Day is celebrated in numerous countries including Australia where F was born, the second of four daughter. She describes her relationship with her mom as strained at best and looks forward to further distancing herself from her toxic mom as they age.

"Mother's Day always makes me feel awkward. I actually don't want to buy her a gift or card but social etiquette dictates that I must. So I buy a small token," she said.

With a cold and self-centered mother, the four sisters were often accused of being "too noisy" and locked out of the house for hours during their mother's favorite soap operas.

"I had severe bladder infections when I was very young that sometimes caused accidents, wetting myself," she said. "I remember my mother taking off my soiled underpants and shoving them in my face telling me *that* should stop me from doing that again."

Her eldest sister was a bully and physically abusive to F during their childhood.

"My mother never intervened to protect me. She said we should sort it out ourselves. It wasn't until years later when my sister became abusive towards my mother that she took notice."

As a teen, F remembers feeling extremely frustrated with her mother. Her constant hypercritical nitpicking had her dreaming of running away or somehow leaving home at the first opportunity. She remembers fantasizing about her parents getting a divorce so she could live happily with her dad. A kind and compassionate man, she never could and still can't understand how or why he puts up with his frigid wife.

As so many daughters of toxic moms do, she tried to find ways to please her mother and earn her affection. She once decided to clean the entire house including vacuuming thoroughly. Anticipating her mother's happy reaction, she was crushed when her mother scolded her, telling her she didn't do a very good job anyway. After her mother re-vacuumed the home the incident became just another quill added to her mother's repertoire of barbs.

"My mother has a habit of collecting every little thing I've ever done "wrong" and then mentioning these things going way, way back. She often tells things I felt were private or embarrassing and mentioning them in front of me to other relatives or family and friends," she said.

F went away to college to become a teacher and in her class were several women close to her own mother's age. These older students praised her gently. Praise was so foreign to her it took her aback. That's when it dawned on her that her own mother was not mothering her, had never mothered her.

She started paying attention to what her mother said and did and how it made her feel. She began to see that her mother was very self-focused. She seemed incapable of taking any interest in F's life or seeing anything good about her. The criticism escalated to include her choice of friends and partners.

A typical conversation:

Mother: "How are you?"

Daughter: "I have a cold but otherwise I'm okay."

Mother: "I have got a cold too, and a running nose. This morning I felt dizzy and my blood pressure…my vertigo…my this… my that… (followed by more me, me, me…)"

This would continue for thirty minutes or more.

Her first job was in a rural area far from her family. It was a relief.

She found a nice boyfriend. When she told her mother they had taken an apartment together her mother accused her of "being a bitch for just pissing off and leaving us."

"Who did I think I was? I didn't care and my attitude as I became older became more neutral towards my mother."

Now married, she is trying to start a family.

"When I mentioned to my mother that we were considering IVF treatments she replied, 'Well, not everybody is supposed to have children. I couldn't believe how cold she could be.'"

By age 29, F realized that nothing she did could remedy the situation. She could not choose to whom she was born, but she could choose what kind of relationship they have going forward. Years ago she cut off all contact with her abusive and toxic older sister. She is having less and less contact with her mother.

"I am over worrying about what other people may think or perceive (of) my distancing away from my mother. My mother had tried to guilt trip me, to encourage me to re-establish regular contact. The only reason I have anything to do with her at all is because I love my father deeply."

She walks slowly down the card aisle in the weeks leading up to Mother's Day, glancing at the beautiful flowers and lush embossing. Each lovely card whispers to her of a mother's love and our deep appreciation of the supportive relationship.

"I read the Mother's Day cards in the shops and the kind and tender words they speak. I cannot imagine or picture how a seemingly normal or loving relationship between mother and daughter would feel. Those messages seem so foreign to me."

CHAPTER 16

When Four Aces Is Not A Dream Hand

TOXIC MOM TOOLKIT:
ACES - Adverse Childhood Experiences

I'm not a scientist, nor will I ever play one on T.V.

In fact, I am SO *not* a scientist for many reasons, including extreme medical squeamishness, and an empty folder in my brain where my multiplication tables should reside. But I've long thought I should have some scientific perspective to help illuminate the fallout from toxic mothering or some really smart analysis of how children are negatively affected when they grow up in a toxic environment.

How *do* people sort out how much their toxic mothers negatively affect their adult lives?

Ask the universe and it will come to you.

I met a new friend for coffee. This man happens to be a saintly sort, the director of a very interesting and progressive homeless shelter in the town where I live. A former attorney he comes across as part professor, part priest, all compassionate caring. Which couldn't be more different than the first impression I send out of "looks good on the outside" but "obviously emotionally limping" on the inside, I thought to myself.

I decided not to hold his brains and confidence against him. Maybe I could learn something.

He's the one that introduced me to the exact information I sought in the form of a Kaiser Hospital study in which patients were asked a series of questions for a project that focused on Adverse Childhood Experiences, or ACES.

In a nutshell, the study focuses on how the number of ACES one experiences in youth can be a point of calibration to predict emotional problems that could be serious in adulthood. My friend values the study as a way to look at the causes of homelessness, which often includes components of emotional turmoil or feelings of hopelessness. Sessions for homeless clients that utilize this measuring tool are taking place at my local shelter and the feedback has been positive.

I, on the other hand, immediately valued the scientific method for taking a person's life story and pulling out the ACES as a way of exploring what daughters of toxic mothers experience. What do I like about it? That by clicking off "yes" or "no" to a page of questions a person could really see objectively that damage was indeed inflicted.

I ran straight home and found the study online and the questionnaire and found that I scored 7 on this test. I knew from my coffee chat that anything over a four ACES was considered the tipping point for bad things including a high risk for becoming homeless.

I think my own internal gyroscope for focusing on the good has gone a long way for helping me rise above my ACES score.

You can find even more information about this study at: http://www.seclinicatcots.org/page12/page12.html

ACES QUESTIONAIRE

Prior to your 18th birthday:

1. Did a parent or other adult in the household **often or very often...**

> Swear at you, insult you, put you down, or humiliate you?
>> **or**
> Act in a way that made you afraid that you might be physically hurt?
>> Yes   No

If yes enter 1   _____

2. Did a parent or other adult in the household **often or very often...**

> Push, grab, slap, or throw something at you?
>> **or**
> **Ever** hit you so hard that you had marks or were injured?
>> Yes   No

If yes enter 1   _____

3. Did an adult or person at least five years older than you **ever...**

> Touch or fondle you or have you touch their body in a sexual way?
>
> **or**
>
> Attempt or actually have oral, anal, or vaginal intercourse with you?
>
> Yes   No

If yes enter 1   _____

4. Did you **often or very often** feel that ...

> No one in your family loved you or thought you were important or special?
>
> **or**
>
> Your family didn't look out for each other, feel close to each other, or support each other?
>
> Yes   No

If yes enter 1   _____

5. Did you **often or very often** feel that ...

> You didn't have enough to eat, had to wear dirty clothes, and had no one to protect you?

or

Your parents were too drunk or high to take care of you or take you to the doctor if you needed it?

Yes   No

If yes enter 1   _____

6. Was a biological parent **ever** lost to you through divorce, abandonment, or other reason?

Yes   No

If yes enter 1   _____

7. Was your mother or stepmother:

Often or very often pushed, grabbed, slapped, or had something thrown at her?

or

Sometimes, often, or very often kicked, bitten, hit with a fist, or hit with something hard?

or

Ever repeatedly hit over at least a few minutes or threatened with a gun or knife?

Yes   No

If yes enter 1   _____

8. Did you live with anyone who was a problem drinker or alcoholic or who used street drugs?

Yes   No

If yes enter 1   _____

9. Was a household member depressed or mentally ill or did a household member attempt suicide?

Yes   No

If yes enter 1   _____

10. Did a household member go to prison?

Yes   No

If yes enter 1   _____

Now add up your "Yes" answers: _____

The total number added up is your ACE Score.

⋙ ⋘

Someone who scored an 8 on this quiz filled out one of my questionnaires. Her story is our next chapter. She is T '89.

CHAPTER 17

So Toxic Even A Kindergartener Knew

"I sat on the floor of our one bedroom apartment watching cartoons and crying. I thought she was dying and I didn't know how to help." – T, born in 1989

T was born in 1989 in a Western state. She was the youngest of four siblings, the third daughter. Her mother was her hero.

"I looked up to her. She wasn't around much, but when she was I wanted to be around her every second," she remembers.

When her parents divorced her brother stayed with their dad and the girls went with mom. After living on the streets, the mom and daughters moved in with mom's heroin-addict boyfriend. T often ran to the neighbors for help when her mom suffered through drug withdrawals, or when the boyfriend beat her mom.

Soon, the line between children and adults blurred. There were some days when a kindergartner played nurse for her mother.

"I sat on the floor of our one bedroom apartment watching cartoons and crying. I thought she was dying and I didn't know how to help," she said.

Her mother was ice cold so she covered her with a blanket. Then her mother started throwing up blood.

"I asked her how I could help and everything she wanted I got for her. Then she yelled at me to turn off the T.V. and to sit still and not to make any movements or sounds. As I sat staring at her I heard the rest of the world going on outside and I knew. I knew my life wasn't normal and that my mom wasn't a normal mom. I was five years old."

⁂

I've read enough of these questionnaires to know that the story wasn't going to get better. But I also realized that T was another example of a girl who was a jelly-side-up kid. This is the term I use to describe the phenomena of accidentally dropping a half made peanut butter and jelly sandwich and praying the dry side hits the floor. With people, it describes someone who hits the floor but gets up again and dusts themselves off. Jelly side down? They're stuck. They feel sorry for themselves. They wonder – what's the point? They slide, usually downhill.

In this case, no matter what happened T just kept landing jelly side up. She just kept trying.

She sought and stopped therapy.

❧ ❧

"It didn't help me… it only made me angrier towards my mother. I didn't want any drug prescriptions, which several therapists offered."

Her mother blamed T for many things including her addiction to drugs, her boyfriend troubles and one very dramatic suicide attempt. When T was 13 her mother kicked her out of the house over a man the mom had met only months before. T lived with her father and stepmother, limping though high school. She moved out of her dad's house when she was 17 and graduated high school with a 2.1 grade point average.

All things considered, I personally consider a 2.1 grade point average a triumph!

"I went to college for one year but I couldn't afford it."

Her freshman grade point average was 4.0. She currently works as an administrative assistant at a construction company and is applying for grants to continue her college education. She recently applied to be a volunteer mentor in her local Big Sister program.

She credits four amazing women for helping her be the adult she wants to be, but she misses a true mother/daughter relationship.

"I thought after so many years, I wouldn't care but I am a girl, and every girl needs a mom," she said.

Moving forward, she doesn't anticipate any changes in her view of her mother. She has no contact with her mother – and T is okay with that. My opinion: she's Jelly side up, I'm telling you.

At my request T took the ACES: Adverse Childhood Experiences test and scored an 8, which opened her eyes even wider. I only wish I had figured so much out by my twentieth birthday.

T is clear about her own priorities and her mother's.

"My mother never knew the true meaning of love or family. She would choose any man over her family any on given day."

CHAPTER 18

Driver's Education

MEMOIR

*M*y mother never believed that my stepfather molested me. She didn't like it when I refused to sit near him. She thought I was ridiculous when I wouldn't get in a car with him. She said I was overly dramatic. That I was begging for attention.

As an adult, when I told her that I had definitely, positively been molested as a child by her second husband she was shocked that I hadn't made that clearer at the time. She didn't remember me ever saying any such thing. She also didn't remember telling me to put on clothes to cover up my chest more around the house – a common demand as I began to develop.

If I was molested she was certain I was referring to an isolated incident. An incident she said I had embellished, if I hadn't entirely made up. Everybody knew what a fibber I was. I was such a Sarah Heartburn. And besides, what men do when they are drunk is not what they are really like.

If he did it, she was sure he was sorry.

I sure wasn't sorry when he died. But I get ahead of myself.

My stepfather was among a group of 40-somethings who played tennis with each other every weekend on the Golden Gate Park courts. He was short and squat and struggled with wildly fluctuating weight all his life. If you saw two photos of him – one when he was slim and one when he was roly-poly - you wouldn't believe it was the same person.

He was married during the time he was courting my mother, who was also married and living with my father. My parents were planning to divorce, but they were so poor that it took time. My mother couldn't wait to be free. She regularly dated her new man, who was richer, well educated and had better prospects than my father.

It didn't matter that my mother had visited her lover's wife several times after she had been severely beaten at the hands of her husband. He was a passionate man, my mother said.

"You're too young to understand, but when I touch him I literally feel electricity," she told me once.

Eventually, she too suffered at his hands. After they were married, nearly every night there was screaming. Often the fights accelerated into physical confrontations, including the memorable Christmas Eve when he chased her around our big, fancy house with a gleaming 10-inch carving knife up at the ready. When I called the police, they found it embedded in the center of their bedroom door.

Many nights my mother would roust me out of a deep sleep and hurry me into my plaid school uniform so we could drive around all night to stay safe from my stepfather. When he left for work and it was safe for her to go home, she would drop me off at school, tired and without my books.

When they were getting along there was always some sort of strain in their relationship. He was banned from scratching my back after my mother determined his hands spent too much time near my "sides." As a couple, they were constantly dieting, or not drinking or "trying to be nice" to one another.

He ridiculed me loudly and often. I was forced to begin piano lessons at age 12 and, of course, I was a very poor student. I was required to practice for an hour a day. Each time I missed a note or hit a clunker, I would have to listen to my stepfather's loud crowing laugh to emphasize how badly I played. After my mother hosted a lavish party for the new neighbors, moving our piano into our foyer overlooking the sunken living room, I quit the piano. Even playing a very simple and short classic piece, something a six-year-old music student could probably play well enough, made my knees and fingers shake. I played very badly, but that wasn't the point. My mother had shown everyone she was somebody.

Each waiting for final divorce decrees, my mother and stepfather moved in together before they were married. She bragged that he bought her a mansion, which was true. Our 14-room Spanish style home did include servant's quarters. My mother delighted in thinking that her tennis girlfriends were jealous. She'd finally moved up in the world.

I always thought he bought the grand house to save his face. After all, how many times could he survive my six-foot-two father opening the door and decking him? My dad, although artistically talented and seriously funny, grew into manhood working "south of the slot" as a stevedore unloading ships on San Francisco's piers. He was from a family of towering men with tree trunk legs that included one bare-knuckle fighter at the turn of the century whose ring name was "The Kike Windmill." My dad had lunch in dive bars every day. He could give as good as he got. I'll never forget the heart crushing sound that followed after my dad clocked my future step-dad. My poor, love-sick-despite-it-all father retreated to the bathroom to cry as he blasted water into the tub to mask his sobbing.

I had begun to dream that maybe my mother and stepfather wouldn't actually make it legal. She might be able to get away from him, I hoped. But one weekend I was left in the care of my brother when they drove to Reno to get hitched.

It was soon after that marriage that my stepfather made plans to visit his elderly mother, an overnight trip to Southern California. Why didn't he take me along for company, he suggested. I suppose my mother was happy that her new husband planned a "father-daughter" trip for just the two of us.

I think I was 11 or maybe just 12. I was a kid who still tucked in her stuffed animals into bed at night with the slim body of a busty 16-year-old. I had lovely auburn hair cascading down to my waist. We arrived at his mother's low-rent one-bedroom apartment and it was obvious that she was not happy to see him – particularly with his pretty new stepdaughter in tow.

They talked and drank highballs at a kitchen counter with their backs to me as I sat on a small couch. There were some sharp words before she went to bed early. We watched TV and fell asleep on the convertible couch in her living room. I remember the foot of the bed practically touched a floor-to-ceiling heat register on the opposite wall, yet he made a big to-do about being cold and kept encouraging me to cuddle. I fell asleep in a knee-length yellow nightgown with little rose buds embroidered across the chest. I awoke wrapped tightly in his arms with my back to his front, my underpants missing and my nightie up around my armpits.

Embarrassed and digging around in the sheets to find my under-pants he told me that happens when you toss and turn the way I was tossing and turning the night before. Then he laughed like he did when I played the piano badly.

His mother came out of her room shouting, insisting we "get out" before storming back into her room and slamming the door. We left in a rush not even bothering to brush our teeth. I felt all woozy and weepy, though I really didn't know why. I started to cry as we got in the car.

He tried to cheer me up, singing snippets of vaudeville songs, making jokes and tickling me.

"Oh Lydia, Oh Lydia

Oh, have you seen Lydia?

Oh, Lydia the tattooed lady.

She's the girl that men adore so and a torso, even more so," he crooned.

He called me grouchy. Then he had a great idea. How about we find an empty parking lot and he could teach me to drive? We drove about half the way back home when he pulled off in a little town and found an empty school parking lot. He insisted I sit on his lap. This nearly put me into hysterics until fed up with my whining he got back on the road heading north to San Francisco.

I don't remember very much about that drive home other than the driving lesson stop. I don't remember eating or stopping for bathroom breaks. He was fuming. I tried not to turn my face towards him. I never did learn to drive a car until I was nearly 40. My mother said it was my choice. That she asked me if I wanted to learn, and I said no. That's why she didn't sign me up for driver's education – *because I didn't want to drive.*

I grew up, moved out at 17, and made a life. I rode a vintage Schwinn bicycle in my Marina district neighborhood and, eventually, I became a scooter girl in my thirties, wearing a leather biker jacket and boys boxers under my skirts. I tore up North Beach on my Honda 150 Elite. I could handle that – no passengers!

Fast-forward to the 39-year-old me dating my husband who said, "No wife of mine is *not* going to drive a car." So he bought me a car – a doozie – a metallic turquoise blue '67 Mustang, which I learned to drive with help from the Sears Driving School.

The Sears instructor never asked me to sit on his lap. I was too big and too tired of being afraid. By then, I was ready to take the wheel.

TOOLS

**"And we should consider every day
lost on which we have not danced at
least once. And we should call every truth false, which was not ac-
companied by at least one laugh."**
-- Friedrich Nietzsche

DANCE

I like classic soul, but you may prefer country & western
music. Whatever type of music makes you happy; add
more of it to your life as a no calorie self-comforter. At
least once a day Dance Like Nobody's Looking even if it's
in your chair or car seat. Music is healing.

CHAPTER 19
Toxic Mom Cocktails

The challenge for grown daughters of toxic mothers who drank is gaining an adult perspective on how much drinking had to do with their mother's past toxic behavior.

I've told this story before: One day my (genius) therapist asked me to describe my mother. When I was a teenager what did my mother wear, do and say on a normal day at home?

My mother always dressed to the nines to leave the house. She was always in full make-up. She was always bathed in intoxicating, heavy perfumes. I've said before, if she could wear furs, cashmere or suede T-straps dance shoes to mail a letter – she would. If she could wear them all at the same time soaked in Joy perfume – even better.

But at home?

There was her full-length pink satin quilted bathrobe with a long belt tied in a bow – not in the middle – but always on the side where the hem met her hipbone. Very Audrey Hepburn.

She had this robe for a very long time. It went from a prized garment to a house-cleaning rag. She wore it every day for eight or nine years, basically all through my teens. At the end it became her hair-dying robe with a shawl of red dye riding her shoulders like a moth-eaten fox stole.

Her jewelry was very important. She never took off her bling-bling diamond wedding set or her Russian enameled cocktail ring and a huge pale green jade and diamond right hand stunner. On a boring Sunday night watching Ed Sullivan on television she wore blush and red lipstick. She spent nearly every sitting moment perfecting her Jordan Almond shaped nails. She moisturized her neck and arms like others breathe. She primped like a movie star. She smoked Virginia Slims, holding the burning stick far from her face between puffs. She believed smoke, not smoking, gave you wrinkles.

My therapist listened with a neutral smile on her face. Then she asked me the following question:

"Did your mother have anything in her hand?"

(This is why we *go* to therapists. Why we pay them *money*. Why, when we are done, we bring them three-dozen roses.)

Me: "She usually had a little pale green glass tumbler, a little drink in her hand."

Therapist: "A small glass?"

Me: "Yes, very small. Maybe as big as a small apple."

Therapist: "And what was in it?"

Me: (I had to think.) "Usually a little white wine or vodka?"

My therapist just looked at me over her glasses.

"She only drank a tiny bit. There were never more than two sips in that glass."

Blink-blink.

Therapist: "Was that glass ever not in her hand?"

Me: Thinking.

Therapist: "Was it ever empty?"

Me: (Clap of thunder realization.) "My mother had a drinking problem."

My mother had a drinking problem!

How gentle was my therapist to lead me along that familiar path that I could only see with child eyes? All of my memories of my mother were formed before I had any ability to discern if adults had problems like drinking or depression or other compulsions or bad impulses. I needed to compare what I saw with my child eyes to what I now understand as an adult.

Not only did my mother drink – honey, she DRANK.

Not only did she drink every day, she drank until she was stewed and slurring. It was so common that it seemed normal to me. It was what I grew up with. When she slept during the day, I thought she was tired. When she didn't wake up, I thought she was extra tired. She was tired, not hung over. A child doesn't really know what a hangover is.

What I needed to learn was that so many of my childhood memories included only half the story. It's not that I wasn't smart. As an adult, a journalist, a chaplain I can spot folks with substance abuse issues at 100 yards. Those observations are not negative or positive; they are just observations that might inform my interaction. They can often trigger empathy and sympathy. As an adult, I won't argue with a drunk. As an adult, I'll let a drunk "explain" things to me but we won't be conversing.

If you grew up with someone who had a drinking problem there are a lot of conversations and interactions that might benefit from an adult re-think. Since my eye-opener with my therapist, I've spent plenty of time wondering if things my mother said in my home were said when she was sober or drunk.

For example, my mother's legendary instruction on sex. She looked me up and down one day and grabbed me by the arm and pulled me into her bathroom. She sat me down on the edge of the tub and she sat on top of the closed toilet seat.

"Here's the thing,' she said gruffly. "Never let a boy touch you here (tapping my chest) or *there* (swatting at my jeans fly). Just don't *ever*. You'll be a lot happier."

Had I known or been told as a child that my mother had drinking issues, what difference would it have made? I did haunt libraries. I might have sought out information on how substance abuse affects families. A school counselor could have told me about Alateen or Al-Anon programs.

There's a questionnaire at www.al-anon.alateen.org that might surprise you. The title is: "Did you grow up with a Problem Drinker?" I started laughing when I saw how many of the descriptions captured my experience. I'm listing a sampling of the bullets, not all.

You may have grown up with a problem drinker if:

- You fail to recognize your own accomplishments.
- You fear criticism.
- You overextend yourself.
- You constantly seek approval and affirmation.
- You feel more alive in the midst of a crisis.
- You care for others easily yet find it difficult to care for yourself.
- You isolate yourself from other people.

- You respond with fear to authority figures and angry people.
- You often mistrust your own feelings and the feelings expressed by others.

How did you do?

Did you discover something?

Is there some time period you need to go back and think about?

Should you spend some time considering this topic and how it applies to your family? If it doesn't apply to you and your mom, could it apply to your mom and her mom?

You can't always figure out family history on your own. It's important to discuss your memories with a trusted friend or therapist.

I've always had a hard time opening up to others – - especially about my childhood. But I've found the more I seek to understand my life and enlist others to help me on that journey, the happier and safer I feel.

CHAPTER 20
The Borg Network

VOICES

"Resistance is futile."
- M, born 1957

What happens when you realize you have a mother from another planet?

For M, who was born into a Jewish family with a domineering maternal side, you experiment with thinking for yourself.

"In the Star Trek series 'New Generation' the Borg Network was based on my family. These are people who think, act, walk and talk exactly like each other," she explained.

"This is a family where everyone is constipated. They support each other's dysfunctions and illnesses. No outside opinions or ideas are allowed. They have a special way of speaking to each other, (using) benign pseudo-therapeutic happy talk with no substance."

"You have to be a 'duck in a row' and 'on the same page' etc., etc."

M is proud of her accomplishments, even though telling them makes her feel like she's a bragger. She had her own advertising agency and owned two small art galleries. She worked in youth theatre for many years writing and directing plays. She was nominated for a Pushcart Prize for a short story. She is a former business columnist and now writes and produces short films.

When she was little her mother endeavored to mold her into her own Mini Me.

"She had a bouffant, I had a bouffant – at seven for God's sake. She was always smothering me, always fussing with me, putting Dippity-Do in my hair, forcing me to wear clothes I hated. It was physically oppressive. I was like her little puppet."

"My father had an affair because he was not happy with The Borg's attempts to assimilate him. No excuse, of course."

Following her parent's divorce, her mother took her to family therapy. Just the two of them.

"The therapist told her point blank that she would have a lot of trouble with me if I didn't get therapy. Her parents told her not to take me. She listened to her parents."

This was when her mother's man bashing escalated. She told her daughter never to trust men. Her mother constantly belittled M's father, saying over and over how much she hated him.

When a family member attempted to molest her, a hospital visit triggered a medical emergency, which further traumatized M.

"My father drove a long way to see me in the hospital and I refused to see him because she constantly told me how horrible he was."

Back home, life, as she knew it in The Borg Network resumed.

Not only was she responsible for cleaning the house, there existed a detailed, structured method for cleaning different areas of the house. Failure to meet exacting standards earned wooden spoon spankings and various thrashings including having a ukulele smashed over her head.

Her first suicide attempt was by taking an overdose of her stepfather's heart medication. The second attempt was a form of acting out after being found out for drinking at a friend's house. The third involved handfuls of aspirin.

Her mother thought dieting might help.

"I learned to pee on a stick and marvel at the color that told me I was losing weight. Weight Watchers was repeated several times. There were lots of suppositories and her obsessing about my bathroom habits. I developed Anorexia and was yelled at for not eating and getting too thin."

She decided she would run away and began plotting her escape by secretly saving money. On the eve of leaving to live with her father her mother stole $700 from her saying it was owed to her anyway.

M left home, got her education, found her way in the world, made friends and boyfriends and, over time, a ballet of sorts developed between her and her mother. The dance always incorporated the same simple steps. Contact led to emotional blow-ups followed by no contact.

"I kept thinking it was my fault. I thought if I tried hard enough she would accept me. She rejected me, then wanted me back, only to reject me again."

"One time she joked, 'I'm Joan Crawford. I'm Mommy Dearest (laughing) mommy, mommy, don't put me in the closet and hit me with a hanger.'"

The more M accomplished in life, the easier it got to have no contact with her mother. Even so, she felt the price was huge and included having her own brother turn against her – for being so cruel to their mother.

Her last trip home was several years ago, and it was an emergency. She had been pressed upon to help intervene with her brother's daughter. M's mother set up a therapy session for the girl.

"It was a disaster. My mother's agenda was simple. Protect her son at all costs even though he was badly mistreating his child. The death stares coming from my mother were better than any horror film. I really fell apart and we fought. She accused me of starting trouble and I accused her of being a bad mother."

"Family members were brought in on a special mission to lecture me. I caught my mother on the phone speaking very badly about me to a friend. She seldom said things to my face, only behind my back. My brother turned his daughter against me. It was hell's soap opera."

Today M has a healthy relationship with only one family member, her dad, who loves and treats her with respect. Part of their bond is the shared refusal to become part of the crazy Borg Network that defines the maternal line of her family.

"My mother is a monster. I have cut all contact, and when she dies I will be happy not to attend her funeral. I know this must sound harsh, especially because of my father's infidelity and what that must have done to her, but I feel no remorse or guilt in saying this. She can have her life in whatever form she needs it to be. I want mine."

CHAPTER 21

Dreams Of Reconciliation: Dream On!

MEMOIR

I was enjoying lunch with a dear former newsroom colleague who also happens to be one of my very smartest friends. She can explain things like video editing or income tax rules without making me feel like a pea brain. So, we get through the salad, the pizza, splitting the bill and she asks if I'm in a hurry.

Yeah right, since when?

And so she introduces the topic we should have been focusing on the entire time instead of catching up and swapping news about mutual friends.

Her mother was dying.

I sighed a little inside because she knows so much about my mothers and me. When had we ever discussed her mother? My friend described her mom as an "unresponsive mother."

"She never seemed to understand that relationships are two-way streets, one was always left feeling inadequate, like you had never done enough, never found the magic words to unlock her emotions," she said.

And yet, my friend was longing for a feeling of connection to her mother.

She was additionally concerned about a sibling caretaker who was caught in an emotional trap whenever others inquired about the mother's condition. Sometimes it felt like the caretaker was being judged on how the parent was cared for. Was she doing enough for her mother some wondered?

My friend felt her sibling was traumatized over and over on top of taking on the toxic mom duty. And like so many of us with toxic moms, my friend was practically leaning forward in anticipation, looking at me as if to illustrate how ever hopeful she was for some sort of mother/daughter resolution before booking that final flight for her mother's funeral.

"What was strange for me was watching myself want to pay my final respects to an unresponsive mother who never wanted to hold up her part of the relationship," she said.

While calculating our tips I offered up my theory on toxic reconciliation. Anyone capable of being consistently cruel, unkind, detached, demeaning or unreasonably demanding towards their own child, is not capable of feeling bad about it - - much less apologizing or offering any explanation.

I think 99.9 per cent of the time: Not... goina... happen.

So I said that.

I could see, just saying that out loud, helped my friend. She leaned back and smiled at me across the table.

Her smile reminded of the moment we met over a decade before. I was trying to look poised while standing in a busy newsroom during my initial job interview. As she walked by, my friend-to-be tapped me on the arm and said, "Don't be nervous. You'll do great!"

What a kind thing to do. But that's what a giving and empathetic person does.

Over our glasses of melting iced teas I walked her through my thought process on letting go of reconciliation hopes. I asked her to consider the years of hurt feelings, the tears, and the confusion that her toxic mother had inflicted upon her. I said, compare that to your own life.

"Having been treated that way, I'm betting you are incapable of being as cruel. But let's say you did hurt someone's feelings once. I bet you felt bad. I bet you apologized and tried to make amends. That's the difference between you and your mother. Maybe it's the one thing she taught you.

A few days later, I received an e-mail from my friend. I loved how she looked at her situation. She told me more about her most recent trip to visit her mother.

"…When I went down to see her I decided I was paying respect to the mother principle in all women, a dutiful daughter move just the same but I felt good about myself after it and have never felt drawn to do anything more. In the end, I tried to be my best self and that has made all the difference. She really had created a narrow world, cut off from all her children, leaving herself alone and wondering why. Finally, I did not feel responsible for that," she wrote.

A lot of adult children of toxic mothers or parents are dealing with the double whammy of toxic parents and their impending deaths. Many seek some sort of resolution while simultaneously dreading end of life issues. It sucks.

It's not easy to train yourself to cut the loop of negative self-criticism that sounds suspiciously like your mom on boxed wine. It's an imperfect process drawing up your boundaries and sticking to them. It's hard getting to the realization that your toxic mom is incapable of making you feel better about your relationship. But be advised – toxic moms like their fish on their hooks.

Many will intimate that some day there will be reconciliation. Some day you'll understand why she is the way she is. It's the hook into you.

Chances are she holds no magic key. She has no confessional letter to deliver. There is no locked box, no speech, no act of contrition she can offer. The dream of a tearful reconciliation is a fantasy. Realizing that truth about this one relationship is how we move forward in the world as a loving and compassionate people. We can have wonderful relationships if we try to trust others and meet them halfway.

CHAPTER 22
Never Marry Your Own Mother

VOICES

"I was in an extremely controlling and abusive relationship with a man nearly two decades older than me. He emotionally battered me exactly like my mother had when I was growing up."
- P, born 1968

To understand why P has emotionally struggled with her toxic mom you need to understand her mother's story.

On her mother's third birthday, her mother's mother suffered a severe fall that resulted in her being confined to a wheelchair for the rest of her life.

"My mom was repeatedly told that my grandmother's fall was her fault. Her mother was taken to an institution where she lived for more than 30 years until her death. Her father shipped my mother off to live with his mother who beat and abused my mother horribly," she said.

Looking back, it is nearly certain that P's grandmother was a paranoid schizophrenic. She was known for a peculiar family motto: "Laugh on Friday, cry on Sunday."

"My mother always repeated that saying, and it kept you from ever really enjoying anything, because you knew somehow you'd be punished. I'm still fighting it and just learning to enjoy little things."

The maternal grandmother is a ghost that looms large over P and her mother. P was born in the Midwest and grew up in a small factory town. Her mother's problems are varied and constant. She suffered at the hands of a mentally ill grandmother who lived above a saloon and shared a down-the-hall bathroom with prostitutes. When P's mother was little, her grandmother turned a blind eye to an alcoholic uncle who molested her at will.

Occasionally P's mother was sent alone by train to visit her father and see her mother in an institution for crippled adults. By 16 her father was dead, and she ran away to live with a female cousin. She married a man who forced her to abort her second baby, over which, as a Catholic, she suffered tremendous life-long guilt. The marriage lasted eight years. He left them when P was six years old.

"My mom says over and over 'You are my only family.' When actually my dad's family is HUGE. He has 11 brothers and sisters and I have 32 first cousins. But I had to choose to be cut off from them to get along with my mother."

As a child P carried the weight of the world on her shoulders. While her mother was as emotionally developed as a teenager, always looking for something or someone to complain about, P worried about paying taxes and losing their home. P assumed the duties of a little adult, housekeeping, bill paying and worrying about money since she was in grade school.

P had few friends and fewer fun activities. Her mother bonded with P's friends like a teenager. Indeed, whenever P visited her father her mother would invite P's teen friends over to keep her company because she was so lonely.

Her mother introduced her to a boy at a grocery store who she dated for nine years before getting married at age 25. The marriage lasted less than four years. In truth her husband confessed that he simply felt sorry for P and wanted to help her get away from her mother. It wasn't enough to build a life upon.

P decided to go to college, eventually earning a Masters degree, and she now works as an academic librarian. She lived with her mother for two years during her college phase, locking herself in the bathroom or her car to avoid her mother's constant smothering presence. During this time her mother married an abuser.

By 1997, although her mother never changed her teen-minded behavior and constant meddling, P had married and was working at a job she enjoyed. Then her world fell apart.

"My heart was broken when my husband, now ex-husband, had an affair. I got a divorce and moved to California with my former fiancé. I didn't see my mom for a year. I actually didn't miss her once during a three-year period," she said.

It has only been through therapy that P now realizes that perhaps she didn't miss her mother because she was living with her mother in a male form.

"I was in an extremely controlling and abusive relationship with a man nearly two decades older than me. He emotionally battered me exactly like my mother had when I was growing up."

She sought out a therapist to work on herself.

"Initially I was there about my relationship with my mother but ultimately it ended up being about my abusive relationship with my fiancé. When my psychologist told me that (my fiancé) was like my mother I literally became nauseous. It was true."

It took six years to end the relationship with support from her therapist who warned her that moving back with her mother, even temporarily, was a terrible idea.

"I only lived with my mom for six weeks until I found a job and an apartment. I was fortunate because I had started to build that sense of self in California. I am currently still figuring out who I am at age 43, but now I am stronger than ever."

She has been blessed to have several friends she can confide in, careful never to "dump" all of her frustrations on any one person. She has thoughtfully studied and practiced the skills required for healthy give-and-take in friendships.

She has reached a point where she cannot tolerate her mother's toxic behavior and is not wiling to play the old caretaker role from her childhood, even as her mother ages and becomes more accident prone and dramatic.

"I truly believe she is mentally ill, and she is not going to change. She has deep issues at 65. I know that I have to accept this, and I do, but I still have weak moments of despair (in) wanting a strong mother. My inner child will forever wish for this."

A note from P 1968:

The summer of my 44th year has been a summer of healing and celebrations. I got married this summer to a man who accepts me just as I am and lifts me up in respect and love.

I am in the best physical and mental shape of my life. I am spiritual and love to take walks in the woods, and long bike rides, soaking in the serenity of nature. I also have learned to foster friendships, and I have more close friends now than I ever have. I am closer to my 30+ cousins, too.

Life is very good right now. I let peace and serenity rule.

After telling my story to Rayne I am less angry. I felt HEARD. I felt VALIDATED. I grieved for the little girl who had the weight of the world on her shoulders and never had the strong confident mother she always wanted. I actually had to cry for her one summer night and some of the anger washed away with my tears. I have boundaries now and no longer tolerate abusive and toxic behavior from my mother. I also have created a strong sense of self finally. I still have a relationship with my mother but I limit my exposure. I still struggle and will be struggling with this forever. I have learned that I can be that strong confident parent to my own inner-child. **I am enough.**

TOOLS

"Know the power of ritual. Release your troubles to the cleansing fire of Spirit. "
– Jonathan Lockwood Huie

CLEANSING FIRE

There are times in life when our only option is to burn items that represent terrible pain. You can grab the matches and a metal garbage can and have your own cleansing ceremony to destroy letters, notes or other bits of paper that your Toxic Mother has delivered to you.

We often hold onto these hurtful documents thinking that we will need them to prove to others how sick our Toxic Moms are. Until the government establishes a Toxic Mom Squad, you don't need this stuff. Keep a hose nearby and let it go.

Safety note per my friend Julie: Be safe. Try not to hurt yourself or burn your house down. Use a metal pail and have a garden hose right there in case sparks from your fire rise up into the rafters. And don't use gasoline or lighter fluid to start your fire. Really. No kidding.

CHAPTER 23

Healing Affirmations To Get You Through

I don't know if you ever do this, but I have a habit of repeating little mantras to myself. These little thoughts or affirmations shield me from toxic mother fall-out.

My friend Jen says affirmations are kind of dorky. I know what she means, but I've compiled a long list of my most often repeated thoughts here. They could you last a month, although I really hope nobody ever actually needs one for every single day.

Here is my version of healing affirmations, sane thoughts, and defense tactics for daughters and sons of toxic mothers:

The 5 "NO" Mantras

- **No**, I won't be doing that. **No**, don't count on my being there. **No**, I'm done subjecting myself to your drama. **No**, I choose not to accept the stress. **No**, I have more positive things to do.

The 5 "I Cans":

- I *can* take everything negative about my mother's life and flip it in my life. I *can* create a welcoming and warm home life. I *can* express love and encourage others daily. I *can* extend myself to those in need without expecting anything in return. I *can* prove that a life well lived is the best revenge.

When Every Day is a Toxic Day: Thoughts to Get You Through

- My toxic mother can't kill me. If she could, she *would have* already.
- Any guilt I feel regarding my toxic mother was planted, watered and tended by my mother.
- If my toxic mother was a co-worker or neighbor and I moved away, I'd never visit or call her again.
- Family secrets instill guilt and shame. Am I being paid to keep family secrets? Then it's not my job to keep them.
- Next time I hear my mother's voice in my head belittling me I'll tell her *out loud* she's wrong. (It's okay. Other drivers will think you've got hands-free.)
- Any mother who could be cruel to a child is not going to apologize to that child when they've grown up. Stop waiting for an apology that will never come.
- As I've matured I've developed a better understanding of the choices my toxic mother made as a woman and mother.

- My toxic mother can only intimidate me if I let her. While she's busy trying to bully the child me, the adult me can reject her, ignore her, correct her, or report her to authorities.
- I can't fight crazy with crazy. Crazy is my toxic mother's 'hood.
- Repeat: My toxic mother does not live in my head. She lives in her head.
- When my relatives and friends say they can't understand how I can treat my toxic mother the way I do, I'll tell them the truth.
- My toxic mother is an unnatural disaster.
- I can laugh or I can cry. I choose to laugh.
- I will never again hand my toxic "mom bomb" the match.
- On Mother's Day, and other family holidays, I'll focus on the positive women (and men) in my life. I'll thank them for their caring, kindness and encouragement.
- The cruel rule of RSVP is that the one person I hope will decline always comes. I won't extend an invitation to my toxic mother to any event where I'd hate to actually see her.
- Mother-daughter time is precious only if it's positive.
- My toxic mother deserves the one gift she never gave me: the truth.
- My toxic mother won't rob me of rich friendships with women who on the surface remind me of her. What are the odds my mother had an even more evil twin?
- I will calmly stare down my toxic mom until she fears me more.

- That which is most personal is most universal. People *will* understand if you simply say, "My mother is not a nice person, but I sure try to be."
- Whose little girl am I? I can be my own little girl. I can care for and nurture myself.

5 Soothing Thoughts:

- Remember what my dad said, "Nobody can resist a joyous woman." Then allow yourself to feel and express joy.
- Consider that your toxic mother may have been treated *even more* badly as a child than you were. (It could keep you from throwing something.)
- There is no dishonor in retreat. Refusing to enjoin battle is a small victory when it comes to toxic mothers.
- Amuse yourself to avoid getting sucked in. Keep an egg timer, a paper pad and pencil near the phone. Tally the lies, the guilt trips and the demands she can make in three minutes. Then hang up.
- Keeping your children away from your toxic mother is a no-brainer. Introduce them to kind, responsible elders instead. Don't know any? Consider visiting or volunteering with your child at a senior center or veterans home for an hour a week.
- Honor thy mother and father? You can honor them by respecting yourself first.

"I close both locks below the window, I close both blinds and turn away. Sometimes solutions aren't so simple, sometimes goodbye's the only way."
From "Shadow of the Day" by Linkin Park

BLOCKS

If any other adult came at you like your Toxic Mom, would you block her? If the answer is yes, block your Toxic Mom on your phone and on Facebook. You can return mail, or erase voice mails without listening, or even build a compound wall around your house if you need to.

CHAPTER 24

The Path To Helping Others

VOICES

"I asked my mother to drive me to a book store when I was twelve where I purchased *The Invisible Wound* (which was) written for survivors of incest. My mother never looked at what I was reading. Never asked why I was reading it."

- P, born 1980

Conceived in a bed of shame, the story of P proves that some kids are just hard-wired to transcend their dysfunctional families.

Today P is a respected teacher with a master's degree in education administration and works with abused children within a school system. She has been honored as Volunteer of the Year in her community and recognized for her work helping people with AIDS. She is happily married with two young children and is done mourning the dream of having a good mother. As far as she's concerned, "God is my father and Mary is my mother."

It's easier that way.

Her mother grew up in an isolated country village in Central America. The custom there was for suitors to come courting with the girl's family hosting a short visit, usually a few days and nights.

"One night my father stayed over to court her and he raped her. She had never had sex before and was so devastated and afraid of bringing shame on the family she decided it would be better if they just got married," P said.

Her father had a third grade education and a growing drinking problem. Her young mother had a year of college but soon gave up any dreams of a better life. They married and immigrated to the United States.

Growing up P always knew that her parents were very different from one another and that their relationship was terribly strained. The mother looked down on the father for being brutish, while the father indulged in every form of family abuse he could discover.

When P was born she became a pawn in a passion play between two sick adults.

"I was always trying to figure my parents out. I learned that my father grew up in a town where his father had many mistresses. He grew up known as the bastard offspring of one of the mistresses. There was abuse between siblings. Once, he came home to find the word 'bastard' spray painted on his house. Our family history is like a terrible book on abuse," she said.

In therapy P realized that her own abuse by her father began very early.

"My therapist is sure my father began sexually abusing me before I was able to talk. At age eleven, another family member raped me. A third rape occurred, but I cannot remember by whom. In school I was an excellent student, and I began to try to understand why these things were happening to me. I discovered self-help books."

"I asked my mother to drive me to a book store when I was 12 where I purchased *The Invisible Wound* (which was) written by Wayne Kritsberg for survivors of incest. My mother never looked at what I was reading. Never asked why I was reading it."

As a young girl P started going to the public library regularly. In the self-help section she found *The Dance of Anger* by Harriet Lerner and learned how to express her anger in a healthy way. At that young age, she understood that her own confusion could become self-destructive. She was searching for a pathway through her own childhood nightmare.

As the daughter of immigrants, she was held responsible for translating the United States at her kitchen table. Her father, a factory worker, required that she translate all work notices and double check his pay stubs. Her mother, who dreamed of one day starting her own business, had the little girl on the phone constantly questioning billing statements, tax notices and installment payments, looking for a way to squeak money back into the family bank account.

"I paid all the bills, wrote the checks. I can remember at age nine, arguing with someone about property taxes. It's why today, I have to watch my boundaries with friends. I usually want to do too much for others," she said.

She started reading the tiny print on the back of bills and zeroed in on health insurance information. She wasn't exactly sure, but it looked like her family had medical insurance coverage should she need psychiatric treatment for her abuse.

"I started asking questions about what insurance covers, and I told myself that, when I was old enough to drive, I could get help."

Her parents had another daughter, a child she came to look upon as partly her own. By then her mother had purchased a small business and was seldom at home.

"She put her life and soul into it, and there really wasn't much of her left for us. My dad began abusing my sister. One time, he had her in his bed, and I just walked in and immediately pulled her out. He knew that I knew. I kept an eye on her after that."

When she told her mother what was going on, her mother called her pre-teen daughter a liar and a whore. A nanny from the parents' home country was hired ostensibly to protect the daughters and keep the dad in check. She promptly began a sexual affair with the dad, who began drinking more and became more violent to everyone in the household.

"There was so much abuse. I remember always holes punched in the walls from him. One time he took an ax and chopped a door open. Chopped the lock off. The police came to our house often. Then the nanny started physically abusing me. My father's paychecks always went to alcohol and women."

Just when it seemed that nothing could get worse, her mother began talking to God. Apparently, God was telling her that her daughters should be punished. They were trees that needed to be straightened. It was her job to make sure they suffered in order to become closer to God.

This entailed constantly telling them that they were bad, evil, not right with God, that they should do more for the family, be better children and mind. A squabble over a toy could yield terrifying retribution. When the girls were "bad," punishment was swift and severe.

P remembers being verbally abused by her mom for asking for a glass of water while at a friend's home. She was pinched until she bled over that. She was told that she should never, ever ask for anything when she was in another person's home.

"Many times my mother made me kneel down in front of a picture of Jesus so she could beat me. If my sister and I were both in trouble she would strip us naked and tell us if we insisted on acting like animals we could lick the salt off of each other's shoulders like burros."

By the time P was 15, her home life was nearly unbearable. A therapist later told her that it was miraculous that she hadn't developed dissociative personality disorder, a psychiatric term that describes what the brain will do to protect itself. In layman's terms, it's when the brain refuses to record any additional abuse, introducing the ability to zone out whenever fresh abuse occurs. It's often cited as the cause for lost memories of very serious abuse.

Adding to the pressure of a chaotic and abusive home life, responsibility for protecting her sister, and maintaining excellent grades in school, P decided to start talking back to her parents as many self-help books had suggested. She began telling the truth.

"My mother would talk about the sacrifices of her mother and father and I would say then how could you verbally abuse me and my sister? How can you allow your husband to cheat and hurt us? And her answer would always be that if I had a better relationship with God, this wouldn't be happening. She would suggest I pray more."

A crisis arose after P broke up with a teenage boyfriend. P felt truly afraid that she might hurt herself in a nearly primitive urge to make the larger long-term pain stop. She cut her wrists, but not badly. These impulses scared her into action.

Through a series of long and intense phone calls, she discovered a sanctuary that offered therapy tailored for teens. She confirmed that her family's insurance would cover treatment there. At the time, because of a satanic cult scandal, the identity of every teen checked into the facility was protected. Once she checked in even her family would not be able to confirm her whereabouts.

"My little sister helped me pack and we hugged and kissed. I remember, the lady that checked me in told me that I was the first teenager to ever check herself in. I stayed there three months."

But the best part of the story is how she got there.

Having never actually driven more than a few blocks in her little town, she grabbed the family car keys and backed out of the driveway. In what can only be described as a miracle, she drove to a major metropolis an hour way navigating a spaghetti stream of on-and-off freeway ramps, without killing anyone or herself.

She parked the car, locked it, and began treatment.

During that time her mother was frantic with worry... and shame. When P was ready she returned home where she was made to pay for embarrassing her family, for shaming them by "running away." For a while, the abuse escalated. But the tide had turned. From then on P had the perspective she needed to survive her family. At school she met a nice boy who would eventually become her husband. She continued to protect her sister while working towards high school graduation and planning for college. All with no support from her family.

By her freshman year in college, her parents were pressuring her to finish her education in three years to save money.

"I talked to the administration about it. I wanted to take more classes, and they felt it didn't make sense. A college counselor told me 'People like you aren't meant to go to school. Pick a trade. Be a mechanic or something…'"

Luckily, one of her professors recognized the incredible pressures she was under.

He encouraged her to stay in college no matter how long it took.

"That was such a kindness and I came to appreciate random morsels of kindness. One would help me survive until the next morsel came along. Even things I would read in books, things like, 'to live is to suffer. To survive is to find meaning in suffering' jumped off the page at me. I held onto these things. I'd think to myself *God put this here for me today to find. I can make it through until I find the next one.*"

In college, her father made fun of her, especially for her faith in God. Her mother told her she didn't have sufficient faith. Her therapist told her, she needed to learn to mother herself.

"I realized that I had to do it for myself. You choose to be a victim or a survivor. Being a victim takes a lot more energy."

Eventually, P married her high school boyfriend. But not before winning a huge showdown with her mother. Not only did P's mother insist that her husband walk her daughter down the aisle, she insisted that the family member who raped P when she was 11 be on the guest list. P's mother was concerned that banning one particular male relative might make people wonder why. After all, nearly every member of their extended family had made good in their adopted homeland.

"So many of my relatives got their education, went on to good careers, and they were all proud of that. We have doctors, lawyers and accountants. At the same time, so many were alcoholics, abusers, cheaters and worse. Nobody wanted to face that."

She stood her ground, had the wedding she wanted, and continued to be very involved in her little sister's life. She started her own family.

She has very little contact with her parents and blocks them from having any contact with her children. Her younger sister views her parents more sympathetically and still visits them, in part because of her sister's protection, which reduced the impact of negative experiences.

P's most recent goal is to become a parent educator to help families like the one she grew up in.

"How do I encapsulate my message? I have to believe even the bad stuff made me who I am supposed to be. I can spend my life criticizing my mother, or I can analyze it objectively to help others."

TOOLS

**"When I got my library card,
that's when my life began."**
~Rita Mae Brown

LIBRARY CARD

If you have a particular issue with your Toxic Mother no doubt someone else went through something similar and wrote a book about it. Get thee to a library and check out books on psychology, mother/daughter memoirs and toxic traps. Look for books and then share that information with others.

CHAPTER 25
When Old Dreams Inspire New Dreams

MEMOIR

*W*hy does the idea of old dreams inspiring new dreams surprise me every darned time?

This is how it goes. You are focused on a dream project – whether a passion, or a research project, or whatever. You commit to do the work – and you burn the shoe leather, and you are proud of the progress you're making.

Then you have lunch with a friend, and suddenly their take on your dream project is quickly summarized into an obvious fact or compelling next step – that you never thought of before despite all the effort and focus you've devoted to the effort.

For example, my friend Jen, the English teacher, and I were having brunch at our favorite patio place in Sonoma and (bless her) she wanted to know all about what my trip to Iowa would entail, so we chatted, laughed, debated what to pack. I thought my best bet would be to blend in by leaving the red polka dot platform espadrilles and liquor tag necklaces at home. She insisted that I have to be my authentic self.

I was finally going to Iowa after wanting to my whole life, not to meet my birth mother, but to see for myself what my life might have been like had my mother kept me (shudder) and brought me back to Central Iowa where she grew up.

Before I could say "Eggs Benedict with the yolks hard please," Jen was focused on my NEXT trip to Oklahoma where my birth mother now resides to finally meet her, or as Jen insists on calling her "The Vagina" to distinguish her from my adoptive mother (Wooden Spoons) and (My Darling) step-mother.

"Rayne, talking about your mothers is SO confusing sometimes," she said insisting that her pseudo-medical nickname for my birth mother would at least eliminate one opportunity for confusion in future discussions.

What Jen didn't realize was that I had already considered visiting my mother, which would take me to a state even less likely to charm me than Iowa.

And yet...

Jen insists that it's really a Bucket List item. A must do.

"Rayne, you came *outta'* her!" she said as the Wine Country sun warmed our brown shoulders. "I'll go with you. A one-day shot there and back. I'll be your videographer!"

Well, that's a new idea and if I think about it and decide that being rejected to my face on a sagging porch in Oklahoma is a great good time – even with Jen as videographer – I'll get back to you y'all.

Right now, I'm thinking probably not.

But who knows?

That's the thing about following your dreams, whether it's reuniting, doing family research, writing a book – or in my case – all three. If you're brave enough to think it, say it, pursue it, write about it and invite others along with you on the journey, maybe Jen's idea will begin to sound logical.

But first, I bought tickets to Iowa, the state that gave us Ethanol *and* me!

TOOLS

"A vacation is what you take when you can no longer take what you've been taking."
– Earl Wilson

ON VACATION SIGN

You can take a Toxic Mom Vacation for a minute, an hour, a week or a month should you decide to put up an 'On Vacation' sign when she unnecessarily contacts you too often. What would happen if you had absolutely no contact with your mother for one week? You take vacations from work, from chores, from gyms. Why not take a vacation from your toxic mother? It is the quickest and easiest method for taking back control of your life.

CHAPTER 26
As Predictable As Falling Leaves

VOICES

"I was very defensive and had a huge chip on my shoulder because my mom was always telling me how different I was from other kids."

- P, born 1954

Every fall, P '54 braces herself for her mother's annual lament about falling leaves.

Her mother, who is now widowed, lives in a 30-year-old trailer in a heavily wooded community.

"She has this little whining voice and every year, like clockwork, she starts complaining about the leaves. They are falling on her deck, (which is about to cave in.) The leaves fall on her car. What can she *do?* The leaves keep falling and she doesn't know what to do…. Like fingernails on a chalkboard," P explains.

She grew up in a little town the younger of two sisters. When she was in grade school her father had an affair that culminated with the other husband – a state trooper - driving his squad car through a plate glass window.

Her mother retaliated by having her own very public affair and, when that imploded, P's mother sort of disappeared, focusing on having her own good time any way she could.

Try holding your head up high on the school bus after that.

When her parents were first married, her mother concentrated on creating the image of the perfect family. She even thought giving an eight-year-old P '54 a blonde rinse was what any mother would do for a daughter with mousey brown hair. After all, her girls were *perfect* girls.

"By the time I was nine I was being treated for spastic colon. The doctor commented that I was his youngest patient with that condition. My mother said it was caused by my over-active imagination and she had to keep me in check," P said.

Her teen years were rough. Her mother told her constantly that P's father – "that SOB" - left the family because P was *so bad*.

"I decided to prove her right. I *was* a bad child. In the sixties I dressed like a hippie in ripped jeans, stepping on the filthy hems. I embarrassed her."

Having little or no good contact with her mother she dropped out of high school when she was 16.

"My mother had no involvement in my life so, why try? I didn't see any future in school at that point."

That same year, she became engaged to a young man who was drafted and went to serve in Vietnam. The young couple decided to part. After that P met another young man who she would eventually marry.

"One day I came home and found my mother burning all the letters, pictures and journals about that boy who was drafted. Since I was planning to marry someone else, she said I no longer needed them. She was doing me a favor by getting rid of bad memories."

Her mother also pawned the engagement ring that P intended to return to the young man when he returned from the military. Her mother broke into a locked box to take it.

By the late 1990's, P earned a degree as a Medical Office Assistant. She has been married for over 40 years and has loving relationships with her spouse, adult children and her grandchildren. Her husband also had a very toxic mom, so he has been very supportive regarding P's mother.

During P's entire marriage her mother regularly visited to inspect her home and criticize her for every housekeeping crime making sure to complain about the general lack of cleanliness of the place and her lack of parenting skills. When P had a daughter her mother was happy. She eventually "took over" the daughter, turning her against her own mother. When P later had a son, her mother called her selfish for even having a son, because it would take time away from her daughter.

Both P and her sister have suffered from debilitating Crohn's disease since they were very young.

"I honestly believe (in a strange way) my saving grace was my sister getting sick when I was 26. My mother took care of my sister to the point where she had no time to pick on me anymore."

P loved her sister. Her sister eventually died.

There have never been periods of no contact between P and her mother. As tough as any contact is, they live in a small town, and P can't avoid her mother for long.

P has seen a family therapist, which she felt was beneficial. She has a strong bond with her husband including their common experiences growing up with toxic mothers. She realizes that her experiences have made her different, although she can't quite put her finger on the exact differences or what specifically caused them.

"I do know that I don't trust people. I always feel that they are just being nice to me so they can get me to do things for them or to make fun of me when I goof up and make mistakes. When I was in school I was a mess. I was the kid that got picked on all the time. I was very defensive and had a huge chip on my shoulder because my mom was always telling me how different I was from other kids. I still feel that way - that I have nothing of any importance to give. I feel that I have nothing to offer to anyone, so I try my best to stay in the background and hide."

"But it's funny, I have a few friends that have come back into my life recently and the first thing they all ask is if my mom is still as crazy and selfish as she was back in the day!"

And each fall, as the air turns crisp and stores start stocking Halloween candy, her mother begins her lament about the leaves falling on her property. P's mother wonders aloud upon whom she can rely to help her with those messy, crunchy, endlessly falling leaves. Just listening to her mother talk about the leaves is "a huge energy suck" for P. It's the annual display of an unfounded victim mentality that annoys P. How can her mother feel victimized over falling leaves - - every damn year?

"Last fall, when she started complaining about the leaves, I told her I would help, but she said that she really didn't want to put me out. I told her no problem. Actually the solution was so simple.

That made her mother curious.

She wanted to know what the simple solution was.

"MOVE!" P said.

CHAPTER 27
What To Pack For A Dream Trip

I had been threatening to pack my bags and fly to Iowa to do research on my birth mother and family and, although *you* may not consider a ten-hour flight to the Midwest with two layovers a dream trip, I did.

Well, sort of.

Having never had a reason – other than conception – to be in the Midwest, I'd been poring over maps and laying plans for a flight into Des Moines and six days visiting my grandparents farm (even if it's a parking lot), my mother's high school (still there, I checked), the library to look at yearbooks for my birth mother's five siblings, and the county records offices to check property rolls. Of course no family research trip would be complete without a trip to the local small town newspaper "morgue" to see what, if anything, put them on the pages.

My adorable and protective husband said that it should be a two-day trip, tops. Sergeant Wolfe said that nobody in their right mind would spend a week in Iowa. I love my husband. He worries about me, and my state of mind on the topic of toxic mothers.

But if I was only going to Iowa once, I needed a week. Any down time could be used to expand, edit, weep over and craft my book chapters. I might actually get some work done!

Coincidentally, a few days prior to my departure, my friend Katherine, the historian, invited me to an author talk at a local college by Abraham Verghese, a Stanford doctor of Indian descent who grew up in Ethiopia.

His best-selling novel, "Cutting for Stone," had recently been the "One Book, One Community" library system choice for Marin County. It's kind of neat. The library and independent booksellers promote one book for a community read and then there are all sorts of events that link to the book. For example, there were Ethiopian food nights at restaurants, Indian dancing at community centers, etc.

Up on stage in a beautiful old theater, National Public Radio's Michael Krasney was the interviewer and he and Verghese began to chat about the importance of geography in storytelling. The main characters in his book are male twins. One grows up in one place while the other grows up in an entirely different place and environment.

"Geography is destiny. They told us in medical school that Freud said that, and I thought that was so fascinating," Verghese said.

Only his medical professor had it wrong. Freud said a lot of wise things but that wasn't one of his observations. Verghese later learned that it was Napoleon who coined the geography is destiny line – and he said it referring to picking your battleground.

I could feel my thinking shift from this dreamy sort of *what if* state-of-mind when it comes to your birthplace to feeling a sort of yearning for understanding how the geography of your life has affected you. It was a topic worthy of battle, a difficult introspective task worth tackling.

As I sank lower in my seat in deep thought I also wanted to sit up, lean over and hug my friend Katherine. She helped put me exactly where the universe needed me to be to plant that thought in my head on the eve of my dream trip to Iowa.

It was a hot night and a full house. By the end of the evening most people were fanning themselves with any scrap of paper they could find. I was feeling warm with excitement that my trip to Iowa was not a dopey waste of time, not another exercise in picking at an emotional scab. No, I thought, my dream trip to Iowa was exactly what I needed to do.

I packed energy, focus and confidence that I have every right to explore anything I want to that relates to my bloodline. My birth family may have kept me a secret in their tiny town, but you know what? A person is not a secret and I had no secrets to keep for them.

How many times have I wondered: Am I the only person I know who has never looked into the eyes of another human being to whom they are related by blood? I have relatives in Iowa whether they know it or not and if I can find one - - even if I have to ambush them in a parking lot - - that encounter could be profound for me. I wondered: Could this trip grant me the perspective to be even more profoundly grateful for my very Dickensian life?

The departure was set for mid-May before the summer heat hit. Dragging carry-on aboard the second connection, I thought to myself: Napoleon was right. Geography IS destiny. The very thought gave me courage.

CHAPTER 28
A Shot In The Dark

"I have probably seen my mother 20 times in the last 25 years. Usually it is for a few days at a time. I have no long-term, absolute estrangement yet, but I am working on it."

- M, born 1973

Born out of wedlock, M's parents married soon after her arrival, delivering her into the bosom of a family loaded with problems and secrets. Her alcoholic mother already had two teenaged children and her father had two children in their early twenties. Her father, who she describes as a raging alcoholic, took an immediate dislike to one of his new wife's sons.

The stepdad beat and belittled his new stepson. The teen became so demoralized he began living in the basement. On the morning of his seventeenth birthday M's mother sent her downstairs to wake her half-brother, so he could see his birthday cake before he left for school.

"He wouldn't wake up. He had shot himself sometime during the night. Things were never really ever the same after this for any of us," said M.

A few years later, her father's youngest son died while in police custody.

"My father grieved hard and drank hard. I had seen him do terrible things as well as really stupid things, but he never, ever hurt me."

By age eight, M was seeing a doctor for not being able to breathe.

"Of course, I didn't know it was stress then. My mother didn't ever listen to me or respect what I had to say in any way. I remember feeling so sad as a child and not knowing why."

She came home from school one day to find her father had left the family. The household was then comprised of a drunken mother, the father's eldest son, the mother's surviving teen son and M. The father's son quickly developed a serious drinking problem.

"I knew my half brother the best and spent the most time with him and we loved each other in our own way, but he was too enmeshed with our mother to be healthy although he professed to hate her."

Though a chronic runaway, M managed to graduate from high school by age 17. She credits understanding teachers for going out of their way to help her succeed, despite living on friends couches and eventually being placed in foster care.

Foster care is hard enough. Imagine having a mother like M's.

"She would pick me up from the foster home for a visit and I would always go back crying because she spent the entire visit getting mad at me. When I was 16 she told me she thought my brother committed suicide because he had molested me. I told her that did not happen. She insisted it did and blamed me for my brother's death."

Not satisfied with simply upsetting her daughter with her sick supposition, she ran it by friends and relatives, creating distance between M and many whom she considered part of her support system.

When she became pregnant with her first child her mother sat her down and told her she should consider an abortion. After all, her mother had very nearly aborted M. She should have, she implied.

"She told me my father talked her out of it. Who says that ever? Who says that to a teen daughter? What do you say? Thanks?"

When M was graduating from college, her mother was surprised. She said she never realized her daughter was smart enough for college.

"I have probably seen my mother 20 times in the last 25 years. Usually it is for a few days at a time. I have no long-term, absolute estrangement yet, but I am working on it."

Almost everyone connected to her family encourages M to show her mother endless amounts of understanding, patience and forgiveness. Everyone, except her father who lived with her mother, and knows better.

Seeing a counselor has helped M. She feels that counseling is never a waste of time or money.

"It is not, however, the fix all of everything. Ultimately we have to decide for ourselves what our truth is."

"I'm done feeling guilty. I took a big step in my healing when I forgave myself for not being the daughter she wanted or didn't want. Basically because of her influence I need to forgive myself for being myself. I don't get a lot of understanding from people regarding the situation, but I really don't need it anymore either."

"Travel is fatal to prejudice, big-otry and narrow mindedness."
– Mark Twain

PASSPORT

They say we travel to find out where we come from. Whether you grab your bus pass, your car keys or your passport, don't hesitate to visit new and different places to help you figure out where and how you grew up. Our passports help us gain perspective, something all adult children of toxic parents need.

CHAPTER 29

Dateline: Dayton, Iowa

MEMOIR

My rental car is backed into a shady spot in the parking lot of one of many Lutheran churches that guard this town. Opposite my front bumper sits the rusty green steel-shed-construction City Hall of Dayton, Iowa.

For the first time in my life I'm visiting the town where my birth mother graduated from high school.

This place has held a lot of power over me for most of my life. Try as I might on the Internet or just squinting as hard as I could at maps, I never felt satisfied that I knew this town. I wanted to walk around this town like my mother did when she was a teenager who found herself pregnant with me.

My birth mother conceived me in the summer of 1955 and was married by November. I was born in February and adopted in San Francisco in May of 1956. She married her sailor boyfriend out on the West Coast and then came back to Iowa to start their "real" family. That's the simple version.

And I'm trying to keep it simple – and not too serious – as I study the landscape and its inhabitants.

This part of Iowa is as flat as a tabletop with farms miles from the next. Local joke: How many customers can a newspaper delivery boy handle? Four. Because all the houses are separated by miles of cornfields. On my trip the fields have just been turned creating huge tablets of black soil as far as the eye can see; each massive field framed by new green grass.

The skies are dominated by enormous dark rolling clouds. They seem to press down on the horizon off in the distance. I find myself driving hunched over, as if I'm racing a clown car across a tabletop with a big wet tablecloth about to descend over me.

I've always wanted to see where my birth mother grew up. In talking to her and extended members of her family, I knew it was small. Heck, the main drag is only two blocks long.

My first thought driving past the Frontier Bar in Dayton, Iowa: *This would be a perfect set for a Sam Shepherd play.* Lots of squat, square brown brick buildings with empty retail space. There were a couple of bars, an insurance office and a pharmacy with dead flies in the window.

But then I saw a vision – *cue angels singing* – there was The Dayton Review newspaper office, founded in 1887. And inside I found a journalism colleague named Amanda who was happy to drag out bound copies of news editions from 1955 because, she said, each year the paper prints the photos of the graduating high school class. Maybe there could be some leads there.

My heart started to race. I was reminded of what my friend Mary Fricker always used to exclaim when reporting got real, "Isn't this *exciting*?"

There were 14 high school graduates in this tiny town in 1955, and I wondered if any of them still lived here. Perhaps one could give me his or her impressions of what my birth mother's life and reputation were at that time.

Amanda, who also understood the value of 'shoe leather' reporting took me next door to the insurance lady, who sent me over two blocks to a man at the lumberyard whose sister just moved back here because their mother died.

He was there and immediately got on his cell phone and dialed up his sister. Would she talk to me? Well sure she would.

"What you want to do is head outta town and go past the golf course and take a right at the first driveway. You can't miss it. She just put up new siding," he directed.

This was the first set of Iowa directions that didn't include a street name or number address. It was not the last. In the days that followed, I became accustomed to folks telling me how to get back on the main road to head south for four miles, then turn east for 6 miles and turn in the third driveway on the left. The first one with camellia bushes.

I drove to the edge of town and soon there she was waiting for me in her open garage with a couple of green and white plastic folding chairs set up overlooking the driveway.

I gave her the Cliffs Notes of my life story and her eyes widened a bit.

What would it have been like to find yourself pregnant in this town in 1955? I asked her.

"This is a town where people don't forgive and forget. There was constant criticism. You couldn't do anything that you could beat home to your own driveway. You'd walk in and see it on your parents' faces. They knew all about it already," she said.

This lady didn't grow up here. Her family moved to Dayton when it was time for her to go to high school. She grew up Catholic in a mainly Lutheran town.

"A girl started a rumor that I was a slut. I was devastated. Then boys started calling the house like mad. I was so upset my parents would hear," she said.

A week later she went out with a new boy who drove her out of town and straight down a dark road.

"I didn't even know where we were. I jumped out of the car and I walked home in the dark. Then they started calling me Virgin Mary. From slut to Virgin Mary in one week," she said.

We talked about my journey, my adoption and where I grew up, what I've done for work, my home life.

"It took me a long time to really own the idea that a person is not a secret. An infant, sure. A toddler, maybe. But who wants to be grown up and be the subject of a bunch of secrets?" I said.

That's when she excused herself for a minute and went back into her house to find something for me. It was her 1955 year book. She wanted me to have it.

"Maybe it might give you more clues," she said.

"You know, I only had one good friend, another cheerleader in school, and I can't remember your mother being friends with anyone," she said. "I do remember she rode horses. Maybe her horse was her best friend."

As I was leaving, I mentioned that my mother had a brother that was killed in Korea, and that reminded her that her own father donated the land for the memorial park nearby that honored that lost veteran.

"It's just two driveways back towards town. It says 'Road Closed' but that's just because the bridge is out and you won't have to drive that far and anyone can see the bridge is out," she said reassuring me that only an idiot would actually drive out on a broken bridge.

I did find the stone memorial on a hill overlooking the spot where the town has an annual rodeo. After paying my respects, I drove over to the high school.

Shoe leather research is funny – it hardly ever fails. People just want to help. The secretaries at the school knew exactly where my birth mother's family farm was, who bought it and when.

"What you want to do is drive out of our driveway and when you hit blacktop that's zero. Then drive two miles south and two miles west," one of them told me. "You can't miss it, he has all those horses in a coral with a big brick barn."

Who gives directions like that? Never any addresses.

Sure enough, four miles later after traversing a raised dirt wall that separated two huge black fields, I was in the circular driveway of my grandfather's farm with the solid brick barn and the 2,400 square foot farmhouse built in 1914. Suddenly, the wind picked up blowing so strongly that mature trees were bending this way and that.

As I pulled my rental car into his driveway, Farmer Green was pulling out with a trailer full of horses to put away before the storm got there. Remember The Wizard of Oz? Like that.

Sure, sure, he said, I could take pictures. And there I stood on the front porch of the house that knew me when I was a secret inside my mother. I was in the driveway my mother traversed when she took a bus to the Bay Area where her husband was stationed.

This was my grandfather's house, maybe my great-grandfather's. These were the same mature trees they saw outside their windows. This was the same screen door. I stood on the porch and walked down the worn plank steps.

As I got in my car and drove away, I felt exhilarated but also a tiny bit weepy that so many people in this tiny community had given so much information to me in a single day. I was brimming over with gratitude.

The next morning, Mrs. Green called back to say come over to the house Monday evening.

"We just got married eight weeks ago, so I'm still trying to blend my stuff with his stuff, so it's a mess, but you can't come all this way and not see the inside of the house your mother grew up in," she said, proving something I should know already.

When you have a dream – even if it takes you to a little old place like Dayton, Iowa - it's your dream, and you can claim it. Nobody was stopping me. All the information I wanted was waiting for me.

"We gain strength, and courage, and confidence by each experience in which we really stop to look fear in the face. We must do that which we think we cannot."

– Eleanor Roosevelt

PUBLIC SPACES

Undercover cops swear by public space meetings. They can create a safe zone and set up surveillance without tipping off a criminal. It is also recommended that you choose a public space to break off your romance. If you have to meet with your Toxic Mom, choose a location with lots of other people around.

Target is always good. No one likes to look bad at Target, so it might keep your Toxic Mother in line. Plus, there are plenty of places to hide in case it gets hairy.

CHAPTER 30
Worst Case Scenario

What would Mary's mother criticize about her?

"Based on what she has said to me in recent years: My humor is mean. My communication style is mean. I am mean. Also, since I don't agree with her version of events, I am a big liar. I am also a bad parent, fat and my political leanings are of Satan."

Her mother would also say Mary lacks understanding, she doesn't meet her mother's needs, she is too quick to forgive herself for things her mother is still angry about, she makes fun of people, and she is stupid.

"I am a slut. I ruined her life. I destroyed her family. I steal. I cheat. I trick people into taking my side. I am disloyal. I am ugly. God hates me. I am bad with money. I am a bad housekeeper. I am lazy and I voted for Obama."

Mary grew up in a devoutly religious home with five siblings and numerous stepsiblings. Her mother was adept at pitting siblings against each other while pampering one chosen child of her choosing.

"As a child, I was her caretaker. It was my job to make sure she was happy, to support her and to help raise my siblings because she was always too sick with new illnesses she read about or saw on television," said Mary.

She was told that college wasn't an option for her.

"What I needed to do was become a stewardess because I had big boobs and my mom could fly free then."

Driven to therapy when her mother accused her of stealing something her mother had gladly accepted money for, Mary showed her therapist a 7,500-word screed written by her mother accusing Mary of all things mentioned above. She also insisted that the movie "Up" was the word of God.

"She let me know that I was bad, everyone hated me and I had ruined her life. Then she made numerous demands. I wrote back saying I forgive her but not to contact me again. My response was just a couple of lines."

Letters from her mother flooded in. Mary's mother wondered how Mary slept at night knowing she was so evil? One day Mary would suffer "godly sorrow" for what she had done. Her mother hoped that Mary would suffer mightily for all her sins.

When Mary's therapist told her that her mother was very dangerous and capable of hurting her grandchildren to punish her, Mary filed a restraining order the next day.

Her therapist asked Mary if she could share her mother's letter with her co-workers as it was such an outrageous thing to send your own child, and there were so many things in it that were examples of extreme mental illness. She and her associates value the letter as the best example of a "worst case scenario" of a toxic mom.

"I didn't show that letter to my therapist to get validation or support. I don't really seek that in therapy. I wanted to stop having nightmares. I wanted to stop having panic attacks at the thought of seeing her. All I wanted was to stop feeling that every time I make a mistake – she was right about me."

CHAPTER 31
Dakota City Synchronicity

MEMOIR

On the last day of my trip to central Iowa, I traveled to the towns of Humboldt and Dakota City, the area my mother lived before leaving the state after her husband died. I had several addresses of extended family, mostly on her husband's side in Dakota City.

One special destination was the town's lovely old Carnegie Free Library, which has been in continual use since it was erected in 1880. Way back in 1979, there was a librarian who worked there who went out of her way to get me Xeroxed copies of a few pages of the 1955 Dayton, Iowa high school year book including photos of my birth mother.

The funny thing was she sent me sheets of photos, which were numbered, but she forgot to include a list of names until a week later. That weeklong gap of wondering which one of handful of girls could be my mother fueled a pretty good freelance story that ran in a long version in the S.F. Chronicle and as a shorter piece for Glamour Magazine.

So, while I was sitting there at the library looking through shoeboxes full of obituaries and binders of birth records, I took a break and asked the current librarian if there was any way to contact my old friend.

This being Iowa, she picked up her cell phone, dialed and left a message at the retired librarian's home. Then I went back to work. I didn't find much other than the anniversary notices for my birth mother's husband's brother and his wife. The town paper ran photos for their 25th, then the 40th and 45th celebrations.

Here's what the Internet can't do for you. It can't show you what a community *was* like. It can't really illustrate how friendly folks are in small towns. It has no chart or graph for how tight a community continues to be.

As part of my dream project to write a book on how to survive toxic mothers, I felt I needed to understand where my birth mother grew up. I needed to consider what my life might have been like had I grown up there too.

So I went to Iowa and learned how folks give directions in these big broad strokes, counting off driveways, ticking off the library, the post office, and churches like everybody-knows-where-that-is for goodness sakes. They do that because everyone *does* know where the old bowling alley used to be. They all share the same landscape that their great-grandparents did.

So it shouldn't have surprised me that, just as I focused on my research, the librarian rushed over to me holding her cell phone towards me. My friend, the retired librarian, wanted me to come to her house six blocks away. So I drove east four blocks and north for two, and there she was.

She hugged me, laughing, and took me into her home where we sat at the kitchen table. Just days before, she told me, she had nearly thrown out her file on me, but something told her to keep every note, every letter now spread out between us.

You gotta' love librarians.

We caught up on my study of my birth family and she caught me up on her life and that of her daughters and many grandchildren. She's a super cool, sharp gal and she confessed that in the early days of our knowing each other by phone and mail that every time my birth mother came in to the library she felt guilty. And she felt guilty often. My birth mother and I both have a lifelong habit of visiting our local libraries at least once a week.

"Of course, she'd want to visit with me, exchange a little light conversation, and I'd be thinking the whole time *I know your secret daughter. The daughter you gave up.* Oh, it was awful!" she said laughing, throwing her hands over her face.

We went through all the stuff on the table and I told her about my visit the day before to my grandfather's, grandmother's and two uncle's gravesites.

I told her, "I had a little talk with my grandfather. It made me sorry I hadn't made the effort to know him. I should have. And he lived to be 92. But even just knowing that in the whole world I was standing that close to his bones was profound for me."

"I stood there looking down and told him, 'I exist. I'm Rayne.'"

She gave me the sweetest look and starting talking about synchronicity.

Synchronicity: The simultaneous occurrence of events that appear significantly related but have no discernible causal connection.

She suggested that by taking a risk and traveling to Iowa, I found so many people that led me to others via synchronicity. Sort of like the universe wanted me to follow ghostly breadcrumbs leading to the truth about my origins.

I mean, what are the odds I'd find the lumberyard man's sister who told me about skating parties there all summer long in 1955? That tidbit connected the dots to a line in my adoption papers:

"(The mother) was practically engaged when she met a sailor at a roller skating rink… He never knew of the pregnancy."

My mother told social workers she was the victim of a date rape at a skating rink and the classmate of hers I'd met only days before was adamant that they all went over to Gowrie to skate.

I mean, how many people can go back to the exact spot – in my case the parking lot of the Gowrie, Iowa Skating Roller Skating Rink – and stand where they might have been conceived?

Talk about synchronicity.

I sometimes wonder, is it always available to us, or do we create synchronicity when we are brave?

My birth mother had two daughters after me, which means I have two sisters or half sisters. The first sister born a year after me looks nothing like me at all, which always made me think that her father was certainly my birth mother's husband, now deceased.

Their second daughter was born a year later. I've always thought that we look very much alike, which made me wonder if my mother didn't go back and have an affair with my real birth father resulting in a pregnancy. Stranger things have happened. That would make her a full sister I've never met.

The librarian offered to show me one of the sister's former homes. On the way back to the librarian's house, she mentioned that my mother's brother-in-law lived a few blocks away. I had been reticent to contact that side of the family. After all, they are most likely not related to me by blood.

And yet, and yet… I felt the invisible hand on my back. Maybe in the future I'll recognize that ghostly pushing feeling as synchronicity.

After more hugs and saying goodbye to my friend, I got back in the little red rental car and headed out of town. As I was driving down a quiet street I thought, *I know this street*, this crossing of this and that. I pulled over. Sure enough in my notes I found an address scribbled in pencil. That little house with the flag in front could be my birth mother's husband's brother's home. Which would make him either nothing to me by blood, or, if my mother's husband was my biological dad, my uncle.

It was late afternoon and I could see a dim light on in the back of the house. I wasn't sure what I'd say or why it mattered as I knocked on the door.

Out came a man I'd just seen in the library's anniversary record book, looking older, grayer, thinner, but smiling. He definitely was my mother's brother-in-law, possibly my genetic uncle.

I was half afraid I'd give him a heart attack so I chose my words carefully.

"I'm the grown daughter that (my birth mother) had and gave away in San Francisco shortly after she got married to your brother. I'm in town visiting and I thought. Well, I thought I'd never be here again so I should say hello," I stammered.

He took my hand. He had the sweetest look on his face. I again stammered, "I know your brother is deceased, but if he was alive, I think I'd like to thank him for marrying my mother, marrying a girl in trouble, because in a way in doing so, he's responsible for me having a pretty amazing life. I can't thank him, so maybe I can thank you," I gulped.

"You should come in," he said leading the way to his living room.

His wife was at bridge club. We sat and talked for a while. He didn't want to say anything bad or negative about my mother. Although he did recall that once he and his brother drove to Des Moines to pull her out of a hotel where she was staying with a man. I have heard from many people that my birth mother and her husband were both unfaithful to each other multiple times.

This man and his wife "stood up" for my birth mother and his brother in Nov. 1955.

"My wife guessed that she might be with child, but you didn't ask and nobody would tell and then they left. You look so much like your mother," he said reaching out with one hand to tap the bridge of my nose and then my forehead indicating that my eyes were duplicates of my mother's.

He wanted me to know that they had two girls and he walked over to a bookcase and pulled out a big blue spiral bound book that cataloged all the graduates of the local community college for decades.

Now, I have seen photos of my sisters. That's how I know the younger one and I resemble each other. He was adamant that I see the photos in the book.

The first one he found was the daughter born a year after me that I didn't resemble one bit. Then he flipped the book to the look-alike sister. That's when he got their names wrong, or so I thought.

Wait a minute, I said. Then we went back and forth until it dawned on me that all these years, I had it wrong. Had it backwards.

The sister I resemble is the older one, which begged the question, could we be full sisters? Could my mother, who confessed to so many interludes in her 18th summer have actually gotten pregnant by her fiancé and not realized it? I wondered if she could see us side by side, would it be obvious?

Walking me to my car, this man stood there slowly shaking my hand. We both had tears in our eyes.

When I set out on this trip, part of me hoped that I would actually look into the eyes of another human being to whom I am related by blood. Having never done so made me feel different from other people who take a genetic bond for granted.

But what difference did it make if my birth mother and her husband really were my parents and that their first daughter was very likely a full sister to me? What had I really learned from all the nice people in Iowa, all the public records, all the headstones?

I drove away feeling like I just might have actually met two relatives that day.

Unbeknownst to me, the librarian had been rooting for me like a supportive mom since 1979. She kept every scrap of correspondence the way a mom keeps her kid's artwork on the fridge too long. She just couldn't stop hoping for good things for me. She is a mother figure to me in a sort of spiritual way.

And the brother-in-law who was so instantly understanding and so kind to me was quite possibly my real uncle.

During my week in Iowa, so many people did their parts to help me come to terms with my origins. Each person, in his or her own way, taught me that DNA is less important than the human connection.

The sun was setting as I drove my car towards the freeway. My eyes scanned the rearview mirror. As if in a movie, I watched the Carnegie Library, the dusty downtown and the ancient Texaco filling station slide across the reflective glass and disappear. I wouldn't see them again. I had found my peace.

TOOLS

"Don't water your weeds."
~Proverb

GARDENING GLOVES

When your Toxic Mom is in your head telling you negative or discouraging things, pull out your imaginary garden gloves and pluck each negative thought as you would a weed. Your mind is your garden. Don't let negative thoughts take root – especially if they aren't really your thoughts but rather part of life-long pattern of undermining and criticism.

CHAPTER 32

Aunt Elaine Says Bee Happy

MEMOIR

Okay, I admit it. I'm addicted to doing research on Ancestry.com. You know Ancestry.com. It's the one with the commercials that feature little green leaves and encourage users not to worry where they are going — to just plunge in and see what they can find. I consider it a bargain at $19.95 per month, and some libraries offer it for free if you have a library card, but you have to sit at a computer station in the library to log on.

They're the people that say, *start with what you know.*

When I began writing this book I launched a research effort on my family. I wanted to be sure I understood my family before I started bragging about how smart I was to grow up happy and sane despite having a toxic mother. I typed in my name and birthday and watched my laptop think. Not only did Ancestry.com find my amended (adoptive) birth certificate, it quickly coughed up my original birth certificate – the "Sally Ann" version – that had been sealed for most of my life, but apparently isn't anymore. My legal birth certificate – the "Rayne" - version has the names my adoptive parents gave me.

In quick order I confirmed the births, marriages and some deaths of my birth parents and adoptive parents. I reviewed overlapping family trees (created by other members) and scanned newspaper obituaries as well as census, military and prison rolls.

I stumbled over my mother's father's newspaper funeral notice where, in teeny-tiny print, I discovered a relative who I had never heard of. That's how I found my adoptive mother's older sister, my Aunt Elaine, when I was 53 and she was 88.

She lived about two hours away by car. I figured the best way to make contact was to write her a letter. Within days we were exchanging letters every day — sometimes two-a-day coming from her. In them she explained she was mostly deaf, had a heart condition and had had several mild strokes. She couldn't really talk on her phone because she couldn't hear, but man, she could write! Her letters were filled with occasional undecipherable scrawls, tons of funny malapropisms, and she always signed off with the directive to — Bee Happy.

She was desperate to have contact with her baby sister, my 84-year-old mother, with whom she had lost contact in the 1970s. I thought it was sweet when she wrote that she prayed for her sister every night. Coincidentally, my mother had been in contact with me, asking me to visit her. We had a long phone conversation about visiting during which I explained that we had had no contact for nearly 20 years because I felt that she was not a nice mother.

News to her, my elderly mother said.

This key conversation between my mother and me was a biggie, because it was the first time I realized that my mother had not only lost her power to intimidate, hurt or upset me. I also noted that her brain had become butter-fingered with any combination of who-what-when-where or why. At the same time, Aunt Elaine's letters had become intense, demanding my constant attention and lightning fast responses.

So, I hatched a plan to reunite the sisters via letters – something they could both do and might both enjoy. *Plus, if I were lucky, neither would remember that I existed.* But first, I wanted to capture the story of my mother's early life. I had to do my research.

If you are in a position to do this type of digging, I say pick up the shovel, baby. Sooner is always better than later. Elderly relatives can be goldmines, but you can't wait till next summer, next Christmas.

You have to do it now.

The point of family research is to gather stories, confirm or reject them, and enrich your understanding of early influences including things like The Depression, births and deaths, wars or loss. So snap stuff up while you can. For those of us trying to make better sense of our early lives, few things are more valuable than old-fashioned fact checking. Start by double-checking your birth date and your parents' marriage date. Counting on your fingers could put a whole lot into sharper perspective.

Facts are the cold waters that drown old arguments.

The crazy thing about my correspondence with my Aunt Elaine was that it quickly digressed to digs and complaints in her shaky hand mainly about my not visiting and not writing sufficient letters. *Well, she is my mother's sister.* Eventually I drove up to meet her, took her to lunch, and listened to many disturbing stories, including her need to padlock her fridge. My favorite detail: she bought things her imaginary visitor didn't like so he wouldn't eat as much and it wouldn't cost her so much to restock "his" fridge.

We talked about her life and when she got married and how her family grew. She told me that she couldn't have children but wanted them so badly that she placed an ad in the local paper, which sounds okay now, but then the police came visiting and told her to stop. She eventually adopted a baby from a lady who already had too many children. Elaine said God told her to drive to the edge of town and knock on the first cabin door she saw. *The detail that makes this story:* Two years after driving away with the baby boy she found at the cabin, safe on the floorboards behind the drivers seat, she got a call from the same wretched family who asked her to adopt another baby they didn't really want – which she did.

This is my family!

It was my Aunt Elaine who told me the story of her alcoholic mother kidnapping my mother from school when my mom was six and then running away to San Francisco. This is a story that my mother never knew. It greatly increased my understanding of my mother's life.

My mother grew up in a family with an older sister and a younger brother, my Uncle Ed, who I have never met. They lived in Farmington, Utah, where my grandfather was a railroad engineer and gone a great deal of the time. The Depression was very hard on the family, but my grandfather always worked and they squeaked by.

When my maternal grandmother kidnapped her baby daughter it wasn't like the cops called in an Amber Alert. In those days police agencies had no interconnectivity. If you needed to find someone in an age when there was no failsafe identification or social security numbers - anyone could say they were anyone - you hired a private detective. While the private dick worked on the case for nearly five years, my grandfather also told every railroad engineer, conductor and employee that he was looking for his philandering ex-wife and his little girl. Eventually, they were located in San Francisco and brought back to Utah to stand before a judge.

My aunt explained that the judge asked my then 11-year-old mother whom she would prefer to live with. My mother's childish choice to stay with a boozy broad ever in search of her next male mark was a sad one.

My mother did stay in contact with her father and brother. Her brother became a park ranger who mailed us little brown paper boxes from his travels. Uncle Ed sent us tiger-eye stones; bear claws and one time, a real rattlesnake rattle. While my brother remembered an aunt that may have visited once or twice, I had no knowledge that my mother had a sister.

Meanwhile, as most good deeds do, this one backfired.

Not only did my mother spurn her sister's epistolary overtures, she was furious at me for setting the postage stamp reunion into motion. To this day, I can only speculate on the origin of the sisterly rancor. Although after my mother died, her long-time boyfriend said that she was ashamed of her shaky hand and could barely endorse checks. Knowing my mother, I'm sure her vanity had a lot to do with her refusal to write to Elaine. Her handwriting would look old. She couldn't have that.

The trouble with family is they are your life's witnesses. I'm sure my mother couldn't stand the idea of anyone exposing her as a poorly educated, man-chasing daughter of a Bar Girl. That I had discovered her older sister probably upset her.

I learned so much from my aunt before she *fired me* as her newfound niece. After months of writing nearly daily letters full of concern and sending her oodles of postage stamps and dime store stationery tablets, she had decided that I was selfish and obviously "in it for the money when everyone knew she was giving everything to her church in her will anyway."

She absentmindedly cut contact with me in a series of nearly identical kiss-off letters. Sergeant Wolfe read the first one and said if I ever wrote to her again he would shoot me and I had to agree. It was one thing to do research, collect oral histories, compile family stories and exchange vintage photos. It was another to accept nuttier-than-a-fruitcake abuse. So I wrote her a final letter full of thanks and well wishes and when fresh letters from her arrived in my mailbox I slipped them in a folder unopened.

Eventually they stopped.

Was I selfish or had I simply realized that I knew how to Bee Happy without her.

CHAPTER 33
Sticks And Stones

"My older brother and I spent a tremendous amount of time by ourselves, outside as wild, feral children. He turned to lighting abandoned homes and machinery on fire, shoplifting, stealing mail and breaking into cars. "

- C, born 1974

Born in Canada, the middle child of three siblings, C finds it difficult to not love her mother.

"She always made sure I had enough to eat, a warm house to live in and clothes to wear both in summer and winter. She wasn't an alcoholic or on drugs," she said.

Her husband sees it differently.

The couple met in college when C was struggling to pay her $500 per month apartment rent with only $550 coming in from a part-time job. Her husband-to-be was her best friend then. Both were studying art. He was the one who brought her food care packages.

He was the one who included her in his own family's activities. He was the first to tell her that her mother was not the nicest mother he'd ever met.

"I watched his family and waited to see the façade of a normal, loving family crumble. I was waiting to see that all this lovely closeness concealed a proportionate amount of anger and dislike. I was so shocked to realize it wasn't an act. There was no simmering rage ready to boil over, no gentle teasing that was actually designed to cause pain," C said.

Her mother saw herself as a savior of children. She gave birth to three, and then fostered three more, including a mentally challenged boy who was with the family until he moved out at age 19.

"The oldest foster boy was removed from the household after it was found he couldn't stop sexually abusing my brother and I. My mother continued taking in strays. They included friends whose own families rejected or were dissolving around them."

Her childhood home was always full, welcoming and had a good meal on the table for anyone who needed it."

Her mother came from parents who never wanted children and reminded their own two of that regularly. C's grandfather had a grade school education but had read every book in the local library and would eventually rise to become an executive for a national department store chain. Her grandmother worked three jobs and ran the household like a ship. The pair fought constantly but loved each other above their own children.

Children were something you did because it was expected and as the grandfather told C's mother and uncle often when they were children, they were only passing through. It was a philosophy that carried through generationally.

A family story concerning C's uncle goes like this:

"A great source of family hilarity is the story of my uncle returning from summer camp to find a new family living in his house. He found a neighbor who told him his family had moved. Did my grandmother tell my uncle they were moving and he forgot? Did she forget to inform the camp? Or did the camp fail to remind my uncle? Who knows? What always sticks out in my mind is the fact that from my grandparents' view this was the most hysterically funny thing ever. It didn't matter that my uncle was frightened and alone, it was 'funny.'"

As expected, C's mother spent her entire life chasing approval from her parents, who didn't give her a second thought. When they visited their adult daughter they told her what awful, terrible, selfish children she was raising. They'd add that because the children were so awful she was a failure as a parent. And she believed them.

Perhaps the disapproval and lack of love from her own parents fueled C's mother into becoming a rescuer of lost children. She opened her arms wide to swoop them in. Too bad she spread herself so thin with others that she failed to provide sufficient love and support to her own offspring.

C's father's background is shrouded in mystery save that he was a British child that survived The Blitz (the German carpet bombing of London during WWII) whose family immigrated to Canada. His parents were known for their habit of not speaking to each other for weeks on end over the most trivial matters.

"My father can whip out some of the most razor sharp cutting, cold and nasty remarks, you might suspect he is high on drugs or mimicking Hitler, or preparing to eat your soul while whistling Dixie. That was when he was in the room. Most of his time at home he spent in the bathroom, especially if there was any conflict. It was like lighting a rocket under an incontinent bear."

There were always great inequities shown to siblings. The younger brother with mental challenges took up a lot of his mother's attention. An older sister, prone to hysterics took what ever was left.

Each Christmas and birthday, beginning when she was a teenager, C received gifts of food saver sets. She would appreciate having them when she moved out, she was told.

"My older brother and I spent a tremendous amount of time by ourselves, outside as wild, feral children. He turned to lighting abandoned homes and machinery on fire, shoplifting, stealing mail and breaking into cars. "

Their mother, who grew up in a big city, said they might learn something insisting they stay outside all day every day, winter and summer. They got to know the neighborhood.

"Two young men on our street killed themselves over drug charges. We had two serial rapists caught behind our house in 'our' bushes. We had a prostitute named 'Love' on our street that my eldest foster brother visited often. One of our neighbors found the bicycle of one of the eleven victims of Canada's most notorious serial child killer behind her workplace."

All of which sounds pretty raw, but pales next to the sledding accident, during which C flew into the air, landed on a snow-covered rock causing severe damage to her back.

"We'd been playing all afternoon and when I hurt my back I told my siblings to go on up home and I'd come along. I was in so much pain, but kids never think pain will last. By the time I crawled up out of the gorge, across the yard, up the stairs to the back door, it was dusk."

When she told her parents she hurt her back, they said she probably bruised her tailbone and would be sore for a day or two. She was not taken to the hospital or to a doctor; indeed, she was chastised for being overly dramatic in an obvious ploy for attention.

"For weeks I forced my body to stand up straight and not bring attention and ridicule from classmates. Easing into a chair took forever. There wasn't one position I could be in that wasn't a nightmare."

She remembers a pain so severe she could hear it, like a ringing in her ears.

"One evening at the dinner table I winced and my mother told everyone to stop and look at me. Obviously I just wanted attention. Over the years I forced myself to believe that it was all in my imagination. The pain I felt standing for longer than five minutes was because I was lazy. I couldn't perform well in martial arts because I didn't work hard enough."

Eleven years later and several years into her happy marriage she finally spoke to a doctor about her back. The doctor referred her to a surgeon who was dumfounded after looking at the X-rays. How could anybody have so much damage and not remember the cause?

"It took me a couple of weeks thinking about it to recall the accident with the sled. I honestly couldn't remember because for so long my mother told me I wasn't hurt, that I was only trying to get attention."

Surgery was scheduled, which was anticipated to take two or three hours, tops. An hour into the surgery the hospital called her husband requesting that he come quickly.

"The unflappable cool-as-ice surgeon came out of the operating theater covered head to toe in my blood, shaking, chalk white and exhausted to tell my husband the damage to my back was much more than they had anticipated. Eleven years of walking around with a broken back required not just one, but two disks to be replaced and two vertebrae fused together to my sacrum in what turned into a seven hour surgery that took a year to fully recover from."

"When my husband called my mother to let her know I came through okay, she casually replied that she knew I would."

Her mother takes no responsibility for eleven years of excruciating pain, the numb shins or the limited movement C suffered for years. She claims that C hid the pain so well, no one could possibly know anything was seriously wrong.

"The angriest I've ever seen my husband always involves my mother. My back operation is something he will never forgive her for."

What do you do with a mother who is cold and exceptionally passive aggressive? What can one do with a mother who prefers to hold onto her own anger, playing the downtrodden saint, waiting until she can inflict more damage with a well timed verbal stab?

If you're an artist like C maybe you try to understand and forgive.

She took her post-surgery back X-ray that includes several Frankenstein-like bolts into bones, mounted it to a light box, and hung it on a wall. She uses it as a kitchen night-light.

When C considered starting her own family she feared that she would model or exceed her own mothers less than motherly behavior.

"I was the person who least wanted children and then it was discovered that I had fertility issues to boot," she recalls of the months leading up to her first pregnancy, which came as a huge shock.

"I cried for three days straight. My art career was finally within my grasp and I was going to jettison that pregnancy like a Fourth of July bottle rocket. I couldn't have children! I would be the worst mother ever! What kind of person brings a child into this world to make them suffer their entire life because I was incapable of loving it?"

But after talking to a friend, who well and truly loved her own children to the ends of the world, she told me simply that I did not have to be my mother. I could raise this child the way I felt was right. And it was as simple as that."

It was 40 weeks of nightmares and fear, but her friend was right.

"Oddly enough, I'm a good mom. I'm an awesome mom. I never knew I had it in me. And no one is more surprised than me," said C, who has since had a second baby.

In recent years there have been several very emotional talks between C and her mother, during which C has laid bare her feelings. Her mother turns it around to blame C for her own imagined feelings of being unloved.

"My mother does not take responsibility for her mistakes. There is no 'sorry' coming from her for anything. But I'm not really sure I would classify her as toxic. I don't want people to dislike my mother – she is not a monster. She's a product of her parents."

Her mother's biggest criticism of C is that she holds grudges.

"She feels I only remember the bad parts of my childhood, that I should forgive and move on and she's right. As I get older I think I'll forgive her more. She is who she is, and I'm not about to change her."

CHAPTER 34
The Beginning Of The End

MEMOIR

I think of my parent's marriage as an escalator; boring until one remembers the sharp teeth at the end.

When my parents finally divorced, the apartment hallway walls told the tale of their marriage. My mother was skilled at egging my father into such jealous rages that their late night fights often culminated with booms echoing in the hallway. My brother says I slept through years of bickering, but the booms would wake me. One was normal, two was bad, and three meant get under the bed.

So many Sunday mornings as I opened my door to make the long walk to the tiny bathroom - the kid's bathroom – I'd pass my dad with a bucket and tools, slathering wet plaster over another fist-sized divot in the wall. The plaster always dried a different color than the paint and over the years, the line of circles grew, punches meant for my mother channeled into the defenseless walls. They were hip high for my dad, eye level for me. His knuckles would still be bloodied, wrapped in cheesecloth, rusty red and oozing.

I never feared my dad in any way. My dad had a wonderful heart. He would unapologetically pat my head with his good hand as I passed. Later, as we settled in for cartoons and Fruit Loops he'd remind us to keep it down to 'a dull roar' to let my mother sleep in.

When my father decked a date of my mothers, sending him flying ass over teakettle down the granite stairs off our stoop, she took the dog with us, leaving dad with only his hi-fi, a movie projector and several spools of Woody Woodpecker cartoons. I think each member of our family ran our eyes or our fingers over the plasterwork every foot or so along both sides of the hall on the final walk out. The tips of my fingers memorized our father's Herculean effort to keep his hands off his cheating wife.

The red headed cheating wife became very old and frail and gray. Her long, golden tanned legs weakened. She tripped on stairs. The second husband – an alcoholic wife beater - died, finally cutting off the alimony gravy train that ran for decades after their divorce.

In our last talk the reporter in me automatically started taking notes of her side of the conversation. Her side of our conversation went like this:

"I just want to talk to you. I would like to be able to see you.
I don't drive anymore.
I'm on oxygen, you know.
Emphysema from smoking.

(She uses her sexy baby doll voice)
I was a bad girl (for smoking) unfortunately.
I bet *you* look gorgeous."

She said…

"I'm still living in my own house (condo).
I've got some girlfriends that say you just can't keep doing this.
I always think I can do it better.
I've got Kaiser."

She takes a long breath and asks me what I do now. She doesn't know that I'm a newspaper reporter without college or much training, just grit.

"Well, aren't you smart? It's exciting isn't it?"

Then she immediately went back to talking about her life.

"I have one cat, a Manx with blue eyes. All white. Sadie.
I'm 82. Can you believe? It's good to laugh about it.
I can't go out walking anymore, it's the pits, it really is."

(She was once thrown off the public courts in Golden Gate Park for wearing men's tennis shorts. They showed her legs off better.)

"I'm housebound. Luckily, I have a *great* place to live. I have trees when I look out all my windows. I live for it. The view."

(Her apartment faced a parking lot.)

"This cat has made me so happy. She's so smart and she's like a little child because she's so smart. She gets mad at me and just turns away."

I ask how long has she been in the condo she bought with the $80,000 divorce settlement from my stepfather.

"Since 1979 – It's the *best* place I ever lived.
I have the best view. I have trees out all the windows.
Did you ever see Don? (Her boyfriend of 30 years, who she refused to marry because she'd lose her alimony.)
He has a beautiful new girlfriend. She's young. She's in her 50's."

"I have a lot of pictures of you and (my brother)."
You look darling in those clothes," she said referring to the mother/daughter shifts she sewed when I was in grade school.

"I wouldn't want to do a whole bunch over, I really wouldn't."

Her voice trails off because she knows I'm not very interested. She's accustomed to having my attention. She needs attention. So she talks about her mother, a subject she knows I'm very curious about.

"My problem with my mother, I'm sorry about.
I couldn't help her enough because she just was so wild.

She was a good woman, but she just didn't know how to live and she was alcoholic.
I know what happened when I was little.
She was doing horrible things."

Her mother, who kidnapped my mother when she was a little girl, was a B Girl, a nickname for Bar Girls; women who sat around bars batting their eyelashes hoping a rube would buy them a drink. She rented tiny back bedrooms within homes and would try to sneak men back to her bed despite sharing her room with her little girl.

"She got the DTs.
Finally they called me to come pick her up.
I had to sell all her furniture.
I had to sell everything.
I put that in the bank for her.
Everything was there for her. I didn't touch a dime.
She got married. The last time I saw her she was in a train, in bed, going to see her family who was going to take care of her in San Mateo."

Only her mother didn't live in San Mateo, my mother did. I realized that at the end of her life when her mind was starting to go, she imagined she had been a normal mother. She blended her life story with mine. My mother had an awful mother. A trampy mother. My mother's mother was as likely to bring home a strange man for the evening as to be passed out on the couch at 3:00 p.m.

I knew how my mom must have felt.

My mother's mother died in a sanitarium after a sad life of rented rooms and Depression era debauchery that included much confusion in their Mormon family over who was married to whom. I was told she often traveled with a male cousin checking into boarding houses as man and wife.

The gift of losing your mind slowly is that normal things, such as television movies about happy families, get confused with your own story. By the time I spoke to my mother after at least 20 years of no contact, I understood that she had truly forgotten that she had surpassed her own mother for misdeeds inflicted upon children.

As gently as I could I explained to her that both my older brother and myself had decided independently of each other to have no contact with her.

Reeeeeeeeeeeeeally? She squeaked in a tiny baby doll voice. She was incredulous.

I wished her no misfortunes, yet I was clear that I would not be there for her at the end of her life. I was at peace with my decision.

She asked in her best imitation of a good mom, "Don't you think that's all bridge under the water?"

I felt a rush of adrenaline pushing me to really let her have it. The litany of her sins against her children I can produce in a nano-second is exceptionally raw. The things she did and allowed to happen to me are the things that they put people in jail for today. I have dual lists of abuse covering both my brother and I. We suffered under her care. How many times had I felt suffocating fear? How many times while in her care did I instinctively scramble away from her feeling as if I was being pulled down under water? How many times did I talk grown men out of focusing on me when she thought they were focusing on her?

There was no explaining to her now that I had found my shore. I crawled up through slime and muck to dry land where I cleaned myself up and led an honorable life.

As a young woman I had contact with my mother, thinking that putting my big toe back in the big muddy river wouldn't really hurt me. It often did.

I guessed that with her mental and physical problems my mother probably shouldn't live much longer. Wouldn't the right thing be to step up and help her, or at least look out for her best interests?

That's when I knew that I was truly an undutiful daughter. I knew the next contact regarding my mother would likely come from a doctor or the Coroners Office, and I was okay with that.

I told her I would not be calling her and that I'd really like her not to call me again. It was the sane thing to do.

I learned later that a year before this rare conversation she had called the police to say that my husband and I were breaking into her apartment to place clothes in her closet. She told the police that because my husband was also a cop, he knew how to break in without leaving any evidence.

Was anything taken? They asked.

"Oh, no they just leave clothes. In my exact size," she told them.

In a way it all made perfect sense to me. She had run out of victims and drama so she invented some.

CHAPTER 35
The Strength Of A Lion

VOICES

**"I was never very lonely again.
Having a lion for a friend gives a little
girl all sorts of confidence."**

- H, born 1956

Around the world there are many cultures that value the spirit of animals and credit them with playing important roles in individual lives. The Native American tribes do, the Eskimos do, Pacific islanders do and so did H, who was born in 1956 to Scandinavian parents.

Her mother was raised in extreme poverty, the tenth child of a fragile mother and a Catholic coal miner father.

"(My mother) talks about her mother with great love, although she'd turned down food that was brought to the door by Mormons, saying she did so to save her children's souls. My mother graduated from a convent/nursing school in Utah. She liked to lie on the couch and read books," said H.

The father of H was raised in chaos and suffered from extreme mental illness most of his life. His childhood was unusual. His mother had died of consumption when he was six months old. His father was a ship captain and gone to sea most of the time.

"He was morose, but very creative his whole life. He was often sent to boarding schools or parked with uncaring relatives."

The third child of four siblings, H grew up in a comfortable suburban setting. She said her earliest thoughts centered on not being loved by her mother.

"I spent all my time on my bike, on the streets, out of the house from a very young age. Fortunately, the streets were not so mean. I drank some, had sexual encounters, joined church groups and theater troops and generally made a spectacle of myself."

Pregnant at 19, she married and moved to a farm home. More children followed that her mother was anxious to care for.

"She seemed greatly helpful, but I've come to realize I should never have left my children in her care."

It wasn't until she had matured and her children grew up that she began recalling many long buried scenes from her childhood. One startling realization hit her like a ton of bricks. She had long buried a scalding accident that required multiple hospitalizations with the Shriners.

"When I was three, one day I looked down upon myself as I was changing my clothes. My memory of the event had dimmed and I genuinely didn't know why, from my right shoulder all the way down my torso was this hideous, rippling scar."

She asked her mother what happened to her.

She was told when she was two years old she pulled a pot of boiling water off the stove.

Memories fluttered in stirred deep within her. She pieced together a broken vision, a flickering movie that takes place in the family kitchen.

Yes, she did have a horrible accident when she was two. She was in the kitchen and there was a pot of clean water boiling on the stove. Her mother was in the bathroom crying.

"My mother cried all the time when she was pregnant with my brother. I must have wanted to help. I pulled the pot off by the handle and the pot hit my right shoulder, spilling boiling water on my neck and face and downward. The next memory is of being in excruciating pain strapped to my bed."

Because her mother was a nurse H was discharged from the hospital early because her mother was qualified to administer morphine.

"I've been told she'd done a bad job because I clearly remember tremendous pain. I'd go to Shriners Hospitals for scar reduction for years."

The next year, when H was three her mother began requiring her to wash the dinner dishes. She would run scalding hot water in a pail in the sink and pull up a stepstool so her daughter was high enough to reach down into the soapy, steamy water.

It frightened H. To this day, she doesn't like having anyone near her in the kitchen, particularly by the sink or stove. Think of the typical family ballet that happens when a big family gets together to prepare feasts like Thanksgiving or Christmas dinners. For H, even people moving alongside and behind one another in a kitchen while holding hot dishes, makes her break out in a cold sweat. She avoids any gathering where guests might be expected to pitch in around a stove.

She won't be volunteering to clean up afterwards, either.

"My mother suggested I'd like to 'muck' in the soapy water like it was a game. But in sequential evenings her tone became sharper. I was to do the dishes. No, I couldn't wait for the water to cool. The whole point was to use very hot water."

The three-year-old tried every way to get her mother to allow the water to cool and her mother just kept repeating, "Get those dishes wasssshed" in a scolding tone.

"I began crying, sobbing, begging my mother not to make me put my arms down further in the scalding water. My hands were already bright red. My father overheard this and abruptly ordered me to come down off the stool. Dad forbade my mother to discipline me and from then on took on the role of my primary caretaker. He became my hero."

Sadly, her father committed suicide in 1981.

What's it like to be a scared, scarred, pigeon-toed, cross-eyed, un-loved little girl? It was isolating. But even a mouse can have the heart of a lion. She was not the first, nor will be she the last child to be saved by her own imagination.

"One afternoon a regal looking lion made his way into the yard walking up from the creek. I watched in awe as he walked up to me and introduced himself. I felt his warm breath on my skin as he nudged my hand, so I gave him a pet."

"His name was 'Ernie' and he was there to be my friend. My friend! My prayers were answered. I had a friend!"

Taking courage from her imaginary animal spirit, H contentedly spent months exploring the neighborhood with Ernie.

He slept next to H in bed and dined at her side munching mud pies she made for him. They walked everywhere together. He even had his own special seat in the family station wagon. Ernie the lion taught a lonely girl to relish secret naps hidden under a blackberry bush, cool against the sandy soil.

"I was never very lonely again. Having a lion for a friend gives a little girl all sorts of confidence."

CHAPTER 36
The End Of A Black & White Life

MEMOIR

My eyes took it in but my brain couldn't sort it out. Was it true that my mother spent her final years creeping around a tiny one-bedroom condo crammed full on every shelf, every surface, every nook and cranny, every black and white photo ever taken of my brother and me as children?

Atop the surfaces of every piece of furniture including kitchen counters were tableaus of an imagined Happy Days life peppered with huge ornately framed photos of my father as a young man; of her imaginary extended family comprised of fellow Costco food demonstrators and their children; and many highly posed moments of herself in better days.

In a way, my older brother, raised me. Most weekend mornings my parents would hand us a buck or two outside the Four Star movie theater. We saw every Vincent Price thriller multiple times and every vampire and Wolf Man and Mummy monster flick sufficient times to mouth the dialog in the dark. Should any eight-year-old know the dialog to War of the Worlds? I did. After the last show, when the usher kicked us out, we walked home in the dark.

Movies were my primary early stimulus, and sometimes I find myself reacting as a character in a film would or exhibiting bravado only appropriate for movies. My brother and I share a common early sixties "B movie" cinematic perspective and when we spoke, we'd speak to each other in that language.

That first day in my dead mother's condo, knowing we faced a long probate process trying to make sense of the mother we never understood, I knew he was seeing what I was seeing *the way we saw things.*

Glittering dust motes floated in slashes of light filtered through cheap Venetian blinds. The effort to gild everything *fancy* stood out in relief: hobnails on leather, pleated lamp shades and the throw pillows she was so proud of, made from gold and bronze paisley velour wash cloths three decades before. Half expecting Alfred Hitchcock to make a cameo appearance as a handyman tapping at the door, we were each imagining the sightlines from her couch, her bed and her dining table. Layer upon layer of her *happy, happy* children with frozen grins dominated every single possible view she had in her living space. Neither one of us had spoken to her for most of her senior years yet there we were, the smiling, the silent, Black and White Us.

Neither of us had seen even a glimpse of her for years, we speculated in part because she didn't want us to see her old. The rare unsolicited conversation or unexpected packages in the mail always left me in a mom bomb fugue state. We had each decided individually that she was too cruel, too unpredictable to maintain a relationship. I often wondered what it meant to have two very different children reject the same mother. We had moved on, but apparently she had not.

We crept back down the dim hallway shooting each other sideway glances as we navigated past the sad still life of her final years.

"How *creepy* is this?" my brother asked.

"It's Baby Jane creepy, dude." I replied.

In the fresh air we laughed and shook off our shock not realizing that this would be one of the last times we were a team.

CHAPTER 37
The Journey From Guilt To Pride

VOICES

"I cannot remember one day when I was not sexually abused, hit or locked in a closet,"

- G, born in the 1950's

She feels guilty that she did not allow her mother to come live with her after her mother's second husband died. And she still feels guilty for not inviting her mother to her wedding 30 years ago. And not a day goes by that G doesn't experience a twinge of regret for skipping her mother's funeral.

"Not because I wanted to go to it, but because I could have been supportive of my siblings."

Her parents married in their late teens and quickly produced eight children, half boys and half girls. She was born in the middle, in the mid-1950's.

"My mother parents' died in an accident and she was raised by relatives who really didn't want her. I realized at a young age that she didn't like me in particular because I was thin and she was not," G said.

Her father was raised by his womanizing father and a step-mother. When the father had a daughter out of wedlock that child was placed in an orphanage until the father remarried at which time that daughter was adopted into the family along with a new stepmother, the infant's mother.

Both of G's parents mentally, verbally and sexually abused their children to some degree. The mother allowed or did not try to stop sexual abuse of her children.

"I cannot remember one day when I was not sexually abused, hit or locked in a closet," she said.

Even after her parents got divorced her father visited his ex-wife's home often and continued to abuse his children at will.

All of which sounds gruesome enough.

Shortly after G's eleventh birthday it was discovered that she was pregnant.

"My father was the father of my child, which I had when I was eleven. I did not realize I was pregnant until my stomach started getting bigger. And even then I am not sure I comprehended it all until I gave birth."

And then there were other men.

"One of the men my mother had to the house was arrested and put in jail. But when he got out, he came straight to our house."

G's mother wanted to be with her new man, so she took G and another older daughter and dropped them at their father and step-mother's home. Then she took some younger children and left town. Eventually, her second husband died in jail.

"My mother left when I was 13 and I never saw her again."

At first she missed her mother. Life was harder somehow with-out her mother around even though she offered no protection or solace.

"She could not love me and she was so mean. As the days became weeks, then months, I kept saying it did not matter anymore. But, of course, it did."

G's oldest sister raised her nephew as her son. It wasn't until G was in her twenties that she realized that her mother was not a normal mother.

After marrying, G sought therapy, not so much to process her trauma, but more as an effort, for once in her life, to have one positive relationship with an older woman.

"I never really talked about my mother or my father. Mostly, I went to (therapy) to have someone who I hoped would be like a mother to me. To this day I still cannot trust anyone, especially women," she said.

Married for 30 years, G still feels nervous about letting her husband get too close. They never had children.

"We have dogs. I chose not to have children out of fear that I might have too much anger inside and I never wanted to affect an innocent child," she said.

Maturity has given G perspective. She says she understands her late mother better but can never forgive her for the way she treated her children, especially abandoning those she left at the mercy of her first husband.

Her son is now an adult with four children of his own. The family has come to terms with his incestuous origins and he is close to the mother who raised him and to G, the mother who gave him life.

She feels great pride that her son has matured into a loving husband, son and an amazing father, supporting his children in all their passions and endeavors.

"He is this amazing person and his wife in incredible. Each of the kids is amazing and talented. My husband and I have taken care of the kids while their parents take an occasional trip or anniversary getaway and we've enjoyed the experience so much."

CHAPTER 38

My Daddy Said It's A Sin To Worry

MEMOIR

*M*y friends ask me how I managed to turn out so normal. Like a lot of kids growing up in less than perfect circumstances, it was the love of one relatively normal adult that saved me – my dad.

My father was perfectly imperfect. He built my brother and me a huge coaster once. He installed a thick black car steering wheel that we could barely get our hands around. Then he showed us where the "brake" was. It was a hinged board under our feet with hard rubber nailed to the underside.

"O.K! Have fun!" he shouted, waving us off.

That coaster was six feet long, made of wood salvaged from his print shop. He used broken up packing crates, scrap lumber, that sort of thing. He hammered thick sheet-metal fenders to the front and top. It was heavy. It picked up speed on hills. It went so fast (even on little hills) that it scared my brother and me. After a couple of blood chilling plunges, we pushed it back home to ask again - - was it really safe for little kids?

"Sure!" he enthused. "I made that thing solid." Then he waved us off again, like a racecar pit boss, refusing to let us refuel or check our tires. We must have hesitated because he added, "Look, if you're really worried, have a kid stand at the bottom of the hill and stop any traffic that comes along."

That was my dad. He told us our family motto was Ignorance & Confidence, which translated into *try without worrying about the outcome so much.*

San Francisco in the '60's was a time when all the young marrieds on our block had as many kids as they could produce without seeming to show off. There must have been 25 kids running through the streets, playing tag late on summer nights, all within a five-year age range and all operating under the sole common parental directive to simply come home when the street lights came on.

So many of our childhood disasters revolved around wheels picking up speed. I suffered the wrath of my mother for weeks after I scraped off the toes of my new red patent leather Mary Jane's riding down 25th Avenue on my belly, head first, on Frankie Fragamenni's new Flexi. Cement can grind the tips of your shoes right off.

One time my brother decided to strap on skateboards, one on each foot, like snow skis.

"Would it work?" My brother asked my dad.

"It might. But how would you stop?" dad wondered.

My brother was pretty sure you could stop that same as you would just using one skateboard. You just sort of turned your feet in until you reached an angle that defeated forward movement. Since my brother had the practical skateboarding experience that my father did not, dad deferred to his judgment.

My brother strode off bravely with two skateboards, two lengths of rope and me to act as the traffic lookout. I was a good traffic lookout too, I insisted all the way to the Emergency Room.

"You said you could stop!" my dad hollered from the front seat of his car as he ran yet another badly placed stop sign. "At least stop crying!"

The pictures don't lie. I was a funny looking kid. I never felt loved by my mother in an open and unconditional way. My dad used to tell me that nobody could resist a joyous woman, so laugh, have fun - be you. For some reason, just knowing that made me feel sort of joyous. It was like he let me in on this cosmic secret. You could make it with enough joy. As I grew up, struggling in high school, looking for work as a teenager, my dad would cheer me on, saying "Somebody gets to work for the New York Yankees, why not you?"

My father was a cool cat. He was an artist, but didn't know it. A character. A good egg. He was kind, gentle and funny. He died of a brain tumor six weeks before our 1996 wedding but he's all around me and always in my heart.

On the day of his second brain surgery, I found a note in my mailbox. It was his rules for a happy life in a child's scrawl on yellow lined paper. After his first surgery he had to re-learn everything including writing, so some letters faced the wrong way, but I could read it.

It said:

Love big.

Laugh big.

Never buy clothes in a bar.

Never bet on a Don King fight.

Remember, people argue because they're both right.

Buy good tools and you'll own good tools.

Never loan tools.

My dad also told me to always throw a big bill down on a bar and let the bartender reduce it over the night.

"That way, he knows you're not an amateur," he'd say with a wink.

My parents divorced in the days when if your dad left, you only saw him on weekends and birthdays. Somehow my dad managed to instill a lot of optimistic qualities in us both, despite our limited time together.

We were jelly-side-up kids. Kids that fell seven times but got up eight. He was one of those adults able to instill so many good qualities in kids without really trying. On bad days, he's the voice I hear encouraging me. On good days, I think *wouldn't daddy love this?*

He created a joyous woman. I think that's pretty cool.

CHAPTER 39

How To Be A Dream Stepmother

MEMOIR

*M*y birth mother and my adoptive mother were each toxic mothers in their own special ways. What my mothers lacked in love, concern and class my stepmother Robbie delivered in endless supply.

I was 14 when my dad married his second wife on April Fools Day. Funny enough my dad also married my adoptive mother on a previous April Fools Day. He joked he feared forgetting an anniversary.

Robbie had been married before. It was a WWII romance that failed in peacetime, dissolving as amicably as two mature adults could manage.

My father hadn't been so lucky with his divorce. He suffered through extended acrimony and spiteful acts, including my mother refusing to let him have his beloved dog.

He was a miserable failure at being single. He found a dark, cold bachelor's apartment. His sole piece of furniture was an upholstered mid-century lounge chair in which he slept. He left it perpetually in the zero gravity position in the center of the living room.

There was the infamous story of the bouncing pot roast – his first attempt to cook a real meal "at home." After that he gorged on Happy Hour food in saloons and drank enough beer to forget that he didn't even own a card table and chairs.

Then he met Robbie in her cute red shoes.

My aunt, who took oil painting classes with Robbie at Vivian Goddard's San Francisco art studio, set them up. Robbie was rather sophisticated. My father was… not.

My father was so broke that he would save up $40 in pocket change over several weeks or months, counting it every so often to see when he could ask Robbie out on a date again.

They would enjoy lovely dinners in pretty places and express affection and appreciation for each other, and then Robbie wouldn't hear a word from my dad for three or four weeks. The third time this happened, Robbie was brave enough to ask why their dates were so spread out. Was he seeing someone else? Was he dating several other women?

My dad was somewhat ashamed that the only thing stopping a fully realized romance was his post-divorce poverty. To Robbie knowledge was power. She immediately came up with a long list of things they could do that cost little or no money. They had picnics, went to the library, enjoyed free concerts in the park, and their love was allowed to bloom.

So many stepmothers get bad raps. Too many earn them. Not Robbie. She took an original approach to making friends with her new husband's young offspring. She simply decided to be a friendly adult and to extend herself when the opportunity presented itself, but she would not court us. She would simply include us when possible.

She bought extra tickets to the ballet for my brother and me and told us during the drive downtown that, of course, we knew the story of Romeo and Juliette or the Nutcracker, but could she share her favorite part of the story we would be seeing, thereby re-enforcing our somewhat shady acquaintance with the classic. Then she explained the timing of the curtains and intermissions; how lights dimming or bells ringing signaled certain things to the audience. By the time we took our seats we had a pretty good idea of exactly what would happen that night, and we were relaxed and happily anticipating our role in the evening.

She bought us books on topics she knew already held our interest. She wrapped small presents elaborately and delighted in hosting dinners, Sunday football get-togethers or birthdays. She never tried to be our mother. She wasn't a mother in the first place having never produced her own children. She simply tried to be a nice wife to our father and to include us in ways that made sense.

When I was 15 she bought me my first real gold earrings and told me that they were extra special and that if I didn't like them to give them back for safekeeping because when I was older I would love them. What I really wanted was big orange plastic ball earrings like Petula Clark wore so I did give them back and she was funny in a good way about it; she was gracious. When I was 25 she gave them to me again, and I *drooled* over the gold paisley drops.

For over 30 years Robbie worked as the office manager for a team of San Francisco psychiatrists in the Medical Arts Building at 450 Sutter, and she taught me to spot crazy at a hundred yards and then to be as kind as possible.

I often describe her to others as the wife character played by Myrna Loy in the Thin Man movies. She taught me that fur was dead by the time you met it on a sales rack, so don't feel guilty for loving it. That there are many pretty things in the world but it doesn't mean you have to buy them all. She showed me the difference between silk and cashmere; beer and bourbon; manners and true grace.

This is what cracks me up about my stepmother. After my father died, she was truly independent but when she needed help she could be demanding. At 87, she was in the hospital for 22 days straight between Thanksgiving and Christmas and it amazed me how often the nurses pulled me aside to comment on how darling she was.

We had a running joke during her time at the rehabilitation center.

"They keep saying, you'll be well for Christmas!" she said twisting her lip and batting her eyelashes and I knew that she meant, oh hells bells, well for Christmas! I just want to get the hell outta here *now* and never come back – she was thinking the entire confinement.

When I delivered her back to her senior apartment complex, the kitchen staff came out to welcome her home, the 25-year-old receptionist ran around her desk to hug her. The staff genuinely liked her.

The receptionist told me that Robbie would often say as she was walking out to my waiting car, "I am going forth to sin!" and they'd giggle about Kentucky Fried Chicken or Chinese food take-out splurges.

Sitting in the borrowed wheel chair wearing a gorgeous purple cashmere turtleneck and black slacks, her simple gold bangles jingling as she shook hands, she reminded me that anyone – even a stepmother - can win anyone over by just being the sort of person who really sees other people and chooses to focus on their good qualities.

Typical of her thoughtfulness, when she first moved into her senior apartment I remember her asking me how I wanted to be introduced "to the other inmates."

"I could say that you are my late husband's adult daughter, but wouldn't it be easier to say that you are my daughter?" she said.

Of course, I agreed with her. Every year it got a little bit easier to be Robbie's daughter.

In 2011 when she was 89 she missed her morning "smoke signal" to the front desk, a rule for each resident of her senior home. If residents don't call in by 9 a.m. they send someone to their door to check on them.

Robbie was found on the bathroom floor, I'm told, in a rather unflattering state, I surmised, although I will never think of her or remember her that way.

To me Robbie will always be the hostess in the glittering caftan, directing my father at the bar and offering up homemade sweet mustard for Chinese food on Thanksgiving. She is with me every time I buy theater tickets or realize I am "an appreciator" of the arts.

The older I get the louder her voice becomes urging me to "buy something pretty" or take off on an adventure or to have enough fun for her too. I'm hopeful that at some time in the not too distant future, she will be the only maternal voice I hear in my head.

TOOLS

"The most wasted of all days is one without laughter."
– e.e. cummings

LAUGHTER

My father used to say, "You can laugh or you can cry. Try laughing." Is there a comedian or classic movie that slays you every single time? Schedule time to have a good belly laugh – even if it's just a YouTube giggle. If you can learn to laugh at your mother's antics – all the better.

CHAPTER 40

What Babies Teach Us

VOICES

"I would never repeat the cycle that I
knew was in my maternal line.
Every decision I made concerning my daughter,
I would think about how I had
been treated by my mother.
How it felt.

- M, born in the 1950's

Her mother was the daughter of immigrants raised in an isolated, hypercritical and emotional wasteland. Her father was simply "the provider" for his upper middle class family.

There were rules and standards of social etiquette. One did not invite others over if it was not your turn. A party included crepe paper decorations and root beer floats for the children. Dinner was on the table at 6 p.m. each day, so father could walk in the door and sit down to a hot meal. Children were seen but not heard.

It was a 1950's Ozzie and Harriet life from the outside looking in, where grades were crucially important.

"I was an 'A' student living constantly in fear of my first 'B' grade. It dawned on me early on that my mother was being very critical of me, without cause," said M.

In her early teens, M's maternal grandmother came to live with the family.

"It created an even more critical environment. It doubled the strength and frequency of criticism for everything I did."

She was told she was lazy. That she had too many boy friends. Perfume was banned because only whores wore it. Nail polish also made her look like a tramp. The policing and nit picking was intense, but never so intense as after her father retired early to bed.

"My mother and grandmother were always questioning me about my social life, lecturing me on the value of being a virgin when you get married… the old 'why buy the cow when the milk is free' theory. When I began to menstruate it escalated. Sex was taboo. I never discussed sex with my mother, yet whether or not I was still a virgin was a common topic."

One statement that floored her as a teen was when her mother told her that mothers are always their daughters' best friends.

"I thought to myself, 'I'm fucked.'"

Throughout her life M has been hurt by her mother's lack of warmth or the desire to listen and see another point of view. She has never once shared a laugh with her mother on any topic or for any reason.

"I don't think I have ever met a woman who so completely shuts out what she doesn't want to hear. She is the most 'black or white' judgmental and angry woman I've ever known."

When M married a man who was not of their faith and only a high school graduate, her mother was angry. She couldn't brag at cocktail parties about the man her daughter hooked, she complained. Never mind that the couple was happy and went on to have four children.

"I know the very moment I realized that I had been short-changed as a woman and daughter. It was when the doctor gently placed my first baby in my arms. The love I felt for him was overwhelming. That love illustrated how much I yearned for a mother-daughter connection."

Her relationship with her mother carried forward into her life, limiting her ability to be friends with mature women.

"I was unable to connect on a genuine basis with my mother-in-law because of my relationship with my mom. My mother-in-law asked me to call her 'Mom' but at the time that was not a term of endearment for me. I still regret not giving my mother-in-law that title. I know it bothered her."

Her fourth child was a daughter. After that birth, M developed a terrible case of post partum depression.

"I was yearning to be mothered and taken care of, for my mom to reach out, understand and be supportive. She was as critical as ever and I just couldn't deal with the toxicity."

They stopped speaking for six months. She wrote letters to her mother that she never mailed. What was the point?

"It was fairly easy to cut off communications. And I felt better," she said.

She remembers a promise she made to herself on the day of her daughters birth. She feels that her babies taught her how to truly love.

"I would never repeat the cycle that I knew was in my maternal line. Every decision I made concerning my daughter, I would think about how I had been treated by my mother. How it felt. I would make every effort to communicate, support and encourage her even if I didn't agree with her. I would let her discover things on her own. I ended the cycle of unrelenting criticism."

With a strong family that exhibits love and mutual support daily, M feels very lucky.

The recent nuptials of her daughter dredged up some old feelings – and some new ones. M is protective of her daughter and her mother knows it.

"My mother criticized my daughter for living with her fiancé (before marriage). Her comments were angry and judgmental, but in a more passive/aggressive way and I felt that old anger rising up again."

She can objectively observe that her mother is becoming more angry and critical as she ages – and she's looking for new targets.

"I try to see my parents about every two weeks, which I do mainly to see my dad, who I love very much. My contact with my mother will be less and less. I want my next 50 years to be free of that crap."

TOOLS

**"Here are the two best prayers I know:
'Help me, help me, help me.' and
'Thank you, thank you, thank you.'"
– Anne Lamott**

PRAYER

It can be demoralizing to wake up each morning realizing that you are or were unloved by your mother. I find praying the moment I open my eyes helps set a positive tone for the day. If you don't pray, try a positive affirmation or take a few moments to think of things that make you happy.

This is my morning prayer:

> "Lord, Thank you for this new day.
> Thank you for the opportunity to do good
> and to be kind to others *and myself.*"

CHAPTER 41

When It All Makes Sense

I was driving home from San Francisco crossing the Golden Gate Bridge into Marin County and I kept thinking *did I write that down?* Did I write down that I hope nobody after me has to wait 20, 30, or 40 years until their own life story of surviving a toxic mother makes sense?

Then something odd happened. I had a gradual sensation of floating above my moving car, then flying above the Richmond District neighborhood I grew up in, then the entire city of San Francisco and I viewed my life as a little speck on Earth. At the same moment the Dickensian epic of my life spread out before me like Bots Dots on the freeway, clear, tangible, logical, connected, heralding a safe path before me.

Here's what I never simply connected until that drive:

I was a baby conceived by emotional strangers who weren't alive enough or moral enough to have any thoughts whatsoever to the future of an unwanted child. *And that wasn't my fault.*

My birth mother did the most decent thing of which she was capable: she emotionally blackmailed a boyfriend into marrying her in exchange for abandoning me to adoption. Not that I'm complaining. *It was the best thing that could have happened.*

Enter my imperfect adoptive parents. My mother was a victim of kidnapping as a kindergartner. She lived with an amoral alcoholic mother, who no doubt exposed her own daughter to harsh neglect and abuse.

My father, whose own cold German father had placed him, his twin brother and their older sister in an orphanage for a year during the Depression and later incarcerated his sons to life without parole (or a decent paycheck) at the family print shop, left my life when I was nine years old. *It happens and thankfully we became friends as adults.*

My parents could not have their own children because my father had only one testicle. My father, not my mother, drove the push to adopt. At that time adoption was considered sad and scary. People from nice families didn't marry anyone who had been adopted, because if you didn't know their parents, their people, who were they anyway? My brother (the offspring of two heroin addicts) was adopted the same year the movie blockbuster The Bad Seed was released. My father's parents were distant to us. They were always much closer to our cousins, who were the same age as we were, because they were their natural grandchildren. These are just facts, and no doubt; my paternal grandparents were members of a big club who felt the same way about adoption.

Whatever love my parents enjoyed early in their marriage was imploding by the time I was in grade school. By the time I was eight or so they were constantly fighting over my father's drinking and lack of progress in life and my mothers sex-driven wandering eye.

I suffered neglect and abuse at the hand of my mother and stayed silent so I wouldn't cause any problems. I smiled and sang and was always a good sport. *So I would be liked.*

Had we been dogs, my parents might have re-homed us or returned us or put us in the pound. Well, not my father, but my mother would have. After divorcing my dad, my mother married an alcoholic wife and child abuser who bought her a demi-mansion. That's where she installed us on our own floor, where we hid until we were old enough to go out on our own.

It never occurred to me at the time that most families invest thought and effort into launching their children into the world; that there is some planning and care. Even if college isn't an option, there is some discussion on job training and careers and where and how to live and what a budget is.

Nothing. I think my father assumed my mother helped me. All that my mother wanted to do was to get me gone.

After a couple of years of being a chronic runaway, I finally left home after my high school graduation at age 17 with $20, a duffel bag with a few clothes, and a blow dryer. I lived with friends and at first I could (barely) pay my bills and hold body and soul together. Luckily, I had a succession of good jobs in financial district brokerage houses with good insurance and benefits and I even traveled a little bit.

Like Horatio Alger I found that working hard worked.

I was this little teeny person just barely making it. I can remember making a box of Wheat Thins last all weekend. I also remember having pangs of envy when people would say that their dad paid off a bill or their family was gathering for a reunion or assembling for holidays. But I never realized that I was essentially alone in the world. Maybe it was better that way.

The calendar pages blew by and the years rolled on and as I drove under the north tower of the Golden Gate Bridge in my mind I was still flying over San Francisco and realizing for the very first time that my parents were dead, dead, dead and truly I didn't have anyone except the people I carefully chose and I curated as my adult circle of friends. In one sense I was as alone as any Dickens poor orphan. But in another way I had learned what David Copperfield also discovered:

"It is no worse, because I write of it.
It would be no better,
if I stopped my most unwilling hand.
Nothing can undo it;
nothing can make it otherwise than as it was. "

I said silently to myself as I drove: "You are just who you are and you are *all you are* and yes, people can be terrible and others can be kind and it's been hard to sort it out but really, *you're okay.*"

After all, I had the ability to love and accept love, to protect myself, to reject those that hurt me, demoralized me or did me no good. I could even seek out answers to family mysteries if that's what I wanted to do. I was lucky that I was somehow smart enough and naturally wired to be kind enough to avoid hurting others, eliminating nearly all adult guilt from my heart.

In the end, telling my story is something I can be proud of. And who knows, if I could manage it, maybe you can manage to reject any fleeting feelings of shame or inadequacy or whatever makes you doubt yourself as the adult child of a toxic mom, too.

As you close this book, I hope you also realize that it was never you. It *was* her.

Toxic Mom Toolkit

Throughout the book we have noted many tools available to us to navigate a life with a Toxic Mom or parent.

Here are the most basic tools, in the order in which they are most helpful.

Safety Glasses – Consider looking directly and clearly at your Toxic Mother or toxic parent's behavior. Observe how the family dynamics operate. Fearlessly study behavior and negative or hurtful activities. I also call Safety Glasses, **Sane Frames.** When your Toxic Mother is overly demanding, guilt-inducing or emotionally blackmailing, put on your imaginary Sane Frames and ask yourself: If any person other than my mother did this, would I take it? You may have perfect vision, but keep your Sane Frames handy for emotional emergencies.

Ruler – Consider keeping track of the frequency of phone calls, visits, letters, and other forms of contact. Don't hesitate to measure all contacts by the toxic individual. Are the contacts normal or abnormal? How do you feel after contacts? The ruler can have a second use. It's it's okay to distance yourself from your parent when they are overwhelming you. Don't we jump out of the way if car a car is coming ...to protect ourselves? Of course, it's self-preservation. Toxic parents dull our responses and mute the inner voice that tells us it is okay to take of ourselves and establish safe zones.

No. 2 Pencil – Draw up a two-column, one page "Pro & Con" document to compare things you enjoy or love about your Toxic Mother to things you do not like about your Toxic Mother or parent. Draw a line right down the middle. Write "Good" or "Positive" on one side and "Bad" or "Negative" on the other. How has she helped you? How has she hurt you? Try to be truly objective. Give her credit where credit is due and track any serious negative incidents.

Shovel – Don't be afraid to dig into your family's history. Have you seen your mother's birth certificate, marriage or divorce records and birth certificates for each of her children? These documents are all public documents and you have the right to read them/study them. And while you're at it, have you studied the maternal line of your family? Very often understanding your mother's relationship with her mother will unlock mysteries about your relationship with her. Don't be afraid to dig! You have the right to understand your family's story. Study as many documents as you can find and talk to elders and family friends to better understand your toxic parent as a person.

Blueprint – After studying your toxic parent's activities, behavior and history and considering the Pro & Con document, create a **Toxic Mom Blueprint** that works for you. It can be in the form of a decision tree --- If she does this, I will do this, then…

> For example: If my Toxic Mother telephones me in the morning I will take the call. If she calls three times, I will take the first call but let the following calls go to voice mail.

The **Toxic Mom Blueprint** is unique to your experience, but can include pre-made decisions regarding communications (phone, mail, visits), get-togethers (family holidays, weddings, funerals, etc.), and access to your children/her grandchildren.

Egg Timer – Keep a kitchen egg timer or other timing device handy if you accept a call from your Toxic Mother. Decide ahead of time, how many minutes you can speak/listen to her. When the time is up, wish her well and say goodbye.

A Mirror – Practice saying "No." in the mirror. "No, I can't." "No, I don't care to." "No, I have other commitments." "No, don't count on me being there." Whatever way you need to say no to your Toxic Mother or toxic parent, practice saying it calmly and firmly. You can say no.

Protective Shields – You may use the same blocking techniques you would choose to block any other negative or abusive adult. You may block your Toxic Mother from viewing your Facebook account or other online activity by adjusting your personal settings. You may block her from calling you on your cell or at work. If it is necessary, you can ban her from your home as you would any other person who is not invited into your life.

Chalkboard – Find a small chalkboard or similar item (any erasable surface) on which you can write positive messages regarding your Toxic Mother. "It's not me. It's her." is good. Or, "If she could kill me, she would have already." Is one I've used. How about, "She is just a woman," to remind you that you have all the power? Positive affirmations can be very helpful when dealing with a toxic parent. You can find lots of inspiring quotes and messages at Toxic Mom Toolkit on Facebook.

Toxic Mom Toolkit Red Wristband – When I landed a job as a New York Times regional reporter I joined a union and I remember getting that card and feeling like I was part of an intelligent, brave and intrepid group. For adult children of Toxic Moms or parents, the jelly wristband reminds us that we are not alone. Indeed, we are part of a large, diverse, brave, wise and funny peer-support group.

Invisible Crown – The trick to overcoming a childhood with a Toxic Mom or parent is to face your own history, gain perspective, assess the relationship, set healthy boundaries and don't apologize for protecting yourself. Imagine yourself wear gleaming crown, having risen above your toxic childhood. When we imagine ourselves wearing a royal crown, we become monarchs of our emotions and develop the discipline to create our ideal and peaceful lives.

The Questionnaire

Questions Every Daughter of a Toxic Mom Should Ask Herself

MEMOIR

*W*hen I was blogging at 8WomenDream.com many readers had entrusted me with their stories, carefully filling in answers to my online questionnaire regarding growing up with a toxic mom.

One day it occurred to me, I should probably fill one out too. Really, how hard could it be? I designed the questionnaire rather quickly, figuring it would take most people an hour or two to complete. When I received questionnaires I was often astounded by the honesty, the heart and sheer bravery of some submissions. Not to mention, the lengths of some reports.

Yeah, I could scoop them up happily, but the time had come for me to put up, or shut up. I wrote an extra-lengthy, very personal post, which originally ran on 8WomenDream.com in August 2010. It wasn't easy. Who knew I would have to consult friends and family about what to include and how to say things?

Who knew I would lose sleep or take ALL DAY to post it? I have struggled with the concept of privacy versus helping others. In the end I self-edited a bit and I decided to save some very hard-to-tell bits for the book – if I'm so lucky to get it published.

After all, you know more than just one of my initials.

I learned through my readers that getting to the nitty-gritty requires some protection, some anonymity. While the original post can be found online, this version for the book includes some updates. I have caught up with all of my thoughts around the topic of surviving toxic mothers in this questionnaire for this book.

I hope this is helpful.

Toxic Mom Toolkit Questionnaire for Rayne Wolfe – born 1956

Q: Tell us about you. What year where you born and where does your birth fit in among siblings? Please provide a basic description of your parents/family. Did your family grow through adoption or foster placement?

I was born in 1956 in San Francisco to a teen birth mom from Iowa who put me up for adoption. My adoptive parents had adopted my brother five years earlier.

My price tag was $2,500, up front. At the time my father, who worked with his twin brother at their father's print shop, didn't make enough money to qualify for a social services adoption. I later learned that *during the qualification period my grandfather would cut false pay-checks for my dad to show Social Services to qualify for the adoption process. My dad would return those checks to my granddad so they could be ripped up. Where there's a will, there's a way, I guess. I was told that I was their chosen child, the child they waited five long years for.*

My mother was a beautiful girl from Farmington, Utah, raised in a Mormon home. Her father was a railroad conductor (sweet and funny, but away a lot) and her mother was an alcoholic floozy from a hard-core polygamous clan.

My mother told us she ran away from Utah, but I later discovered that her mother who brought her to San Francisco to lead a life of debauchery had actually kidnapped her. I know my mother suffered.

My father was raised in San Francisco during the Depression by a stern, domineering German-American father and a gorgeous, lovely, but quiet Christian Scientist mother. When they were eight years old their father "parked" them and their older sister in an orphanage while he looked for work. The "boys" worked for my grandfather at the print shop all their lives.

My brother and I grew up in the print shop: me playing in a barrel of punch holes and making paper doll furniture, my brother riding his Schwinn around the cavernous warehouse and raiding the Coke machine.

My father was a very talented artist and cartoonist at a young age.

A defining incident of my dad's young life was a terrible accident at the shop.

People have no idea how dangerous print shops of that era were with all of the cutting and chopping, the hot glue, etc.… One day a narrow, but long, circular saw snapped and began whipping in arcs and instinctively my father grabbed for it, chopping four of his own fingers off.

The ink poisoned the exposed flesh and microsurgery was not yet invented. Indeed, they went to a second hospital's emergency room when the first doctor proceeded to make plans to cut off my dad's entire hand.

The fingers were thrown away by the second hospital; each finger stub was rather roughly clamped shut and for the rest of his life my dad had four very stubby stubs on one hand. Strangely enough the fingernails continued to grow but they grew out from the center of each tip looking exactly like black dog nails. I loved my father's injured hand, for some odd reason.

They say character is defined by how you react to life's setbacks. My father's recuperation included considerable bed rest. He asked his mother to get him a roll of paper. A BIG one. She went to a butcher shop and bought a roll of coarse brown wrapping paper. My father filled the entire thing re-training himself to draw with his left hand. We have a section of dog cartoons he did left-handed framed. It hangs in my office.

He was happy to draw and do creative things with his hands all his life. He also taught himself magic tricks to regain some fluidity in his mangled hand. Many friends didn't notice his loss for years and were startled to learn that his accident occurred many years before when he was a teen. He could palm anything from dice to a champagne cork and never lost a round of Which Hand Is It In?

My Father and Mother

My mother's early life was overshadowed by her mother's immoral life. A red wine alcoholic she often traveled with men registering at hotels as a married couple. When my mother met my dad she was a high school dropout, working downtown and spending all her free time at the movies to avoid her mother. On my parents wedding day she spent the morning checking her mother into a sanitarium to dry out and the afternoon celebrating her nuptials.

Q: Describe the arc of your academic and professional life to present. What is your current occupation? If you volunteer in your community, how often? Doing what?

I attended a private Catholic girls' high school because my mother decided it was the best private school in the city because it was right across the street and there were NO BOYS.

I was neither Catholic nor happy at that school. My parents had di-vorced and my mother was dragging my brother and me through her horrible second marriage to an alcoholic wife beater and verbal abuser.

We lived in a beautiful Spanish style 14-room home, yes, but it was a hell house for my brother and me. The environment was so volatile none of us ever invited anyone over. Indeed, my first serious boyfriend was a 22-year-old S.F. cop who had been called to the house during a night of domestic violence involving a butcher knife rampage. I was 16 when we began dating and he became my knight — always available to sweep me up and protect me. My mother once threatened to report him to his bosses (for dating a teenager) and he said, "Please do that so I can tell my bosses about you and your husband." I loved that guy.

My brother, our father, and me

Because of the many sleepless nights, the stress of my home environment, I went from being a rather good student in public middle school to a failing ghost at my new high school. I skipped classes most of the time, preferring to lie on the school library carpeted floor, reading away my days. (When I was younger I regularly carried adult books about trying to impress my teachers.)

In my junior year my mother gave me a red set of American Tourister luggage for Christmas explaining that I'd have to get going, get on with my life when I turned 18. I had no idea what to do or where to go.

It's hard to believe in our current environment of parental microman-agement of the road to college, there was never any discussion of college. My school counselor, after spending about ten minutes with me, sug-gested I'd be happiest working in retail.

My first job was as a file clerk at the Pacific Stock Exchange. Remember the last scene in Raiders of the Lost Ark? The huge warehouse with all the crates marked Top Secret as far as the eye could see? The exchange had filing rooms kind of like that with filing cabinets taller than me. I was so happy working — alphabetizing. My boss said he could always find me by listening for me singing Patsy Cline song to myself.

I shared an apartment with a girlfriend and paid my bills and dated and I was super happy on my own.

The stock exchange is where I learned the value of working hard in a meritocracy. I kept my head down and worked my way up to a posi-tion of trust, a listing representative in the marketing department at the exchange. Later, I took jobs at brokerage houses and was usually the youngest and often the first girl to work in many trading rooms on Montgomery Street. During this time I inquired about college, took a few courses at City College, and UC Berkeley extension (earning all A's) but never had the focus or the resources to really apply myself. I didn't believe I was college material.

When a Vice President of the stock exchange was recruited to be a head-hunting partner, he recruited me to be his research assistant. That was one of the most amazing miracles of my life. Someone actually recognized that I had a brain. I spent a dozen years in global, high-ranking executive search, eventually becoming director of research for a boutique firm. Over my 13-year tenure I met thousands of business leaders, developing perspective on what makes people good hires — mainly a decent brain and good character.

My first literary reading IN SUNGLASSES!

Identifying a skill I didn't realize I possessed, my boss encouraged me to become a freelance writer and paid for all my early writing courses. He became a second father to me, encouraging me always. I had amazing success selling everything I wrote. I parlayed freelancing into my own self-syndicated business column in several major newspapers including the S.F. Chronicle and Seattle Times, sharing what I'd learned in recruiting. That led to my first reporting job with a New York Times regional newspaper, where I spent a decade writing the first draft of history for my community.

I have been a business columnist, a business reporter, a community reporter covering philanthropy and volunteering at a daily paper, as well as a top ten blogger for the newspaper I left in 2009 to commence this book project.

I've taught writing and have become a decent public speaker after spending most of my life grateful for jobs because I thought I was kind of dumb. I have always been a voracious reader, a self-educated autodidact.

In a way, my life has been my education.

I volunteered in my community as a law enforcement chaplain for five years, helping the police deliver death notifications. It's a terribly hard task requiring significant training. When I was a reporter I covered volunteering and I felt that my stories went a long way to marshal community support. I was a key contributor (via my reporting) to raising several million dollars to build a new children's home, for example. I specifically chose stories that I thought would do the most good.

Q: Describe the relationship with your mother in three segments: as a child, a teen and young adult.

My mother/early 1950's

My mother (meaning my adoptive mother who raised me) was beautiful, wore furs if she could, red lipstick, and Joy perfume and hypnotized me visually when I was a child. She was warm and soft and I enjoyed nothing more than sitting in her lap with her silk lined camel coat wrapped around us, snug. I enjoyed a long period of just adoring my mother, up until I was about 5 or 6.

By the time I was eight my parent's marriage was on the rocks because of my mother's constant shopping for a (new) rich husband, aggravated by my fathers increased drinking. They fought a lot in our small flat. I was left in my brother's care most of the time. I began to see that my mother had mostly "not nice" days.

My brother and I in Golden Gate Park

Like kids of that era, we spent every waking moment outdoors. But that wasn't enough for my mother. She would lock us out of the house to sleep — I realize now it was because of drinking and depression — but at the time I thought she didn't love us anymore.

I had to shake her awake and beg her to feed us, which she would do only very reluctantly making us Cream of Wheat for dinner or tossing us a slice of baloney for breakfast, whatever was handy. On many days we'd have to show her that our hands were shaking before she'd feed us.

She punished us by breaking wooden spoons on our legs, then slapping us when she couldn't find more wooden spoons. She was unpredictable. My brother and I suffered in silence.

It amazes me that neither of us ever complained to our father, relatives or neighbors. It was like we didn't want to rat her out.

She also did this thing we called "flipping" our lips. My mother was maniacal about buffing and polishing her nails, which were perfectly formed ovals like Jordan Almond candy. To this day I can't use "her" colors — pale mauves, peaches and rusts — on my nails.

This is what flipping is: Imagine there's a crumb on the table. It's a big crumb and you plan to flip it with just the tip of your middle finger to send it flying as far as it can possibly go. You put a lot of force, a bit of snap as the finger pops from the thumb. That's what my mother would do to our lips with her big, shiny nails. Sometimes we'd move defensively and she'd catch our noses, which hurt more.

My mother and me/mid-1960's

My mother's second marriage was violent from Day One but it began truly breaking down when I was in high school. She found a way to blame me. After all, if I had been nicer, he would have stayed. This was my mothers twisted way of weaving our misfortunes into her misfortunes. My mother started to complain that I walked around the house too much and looked trampy. (I was a 32D by sophomore year.) She refused to buy me any clothes other than my school uniform. Any clothes I had for play were my older brother's old jeans or t-shirts, which I tailored down by hand.

My grandmother (my father's mother) eventually took me shopping for brassieres — a true kindness on her part. She took me to City of Paris annually for bra shopping. It was she who paid for made to order bras for me until I left home.

Our demi-mansion had an upstairs suite: two large bedrooms across a landing with a connected bathroom. By high school my brother and I each stayed in our rooms with the doors locked most of the time. If one went downstairs for any reason, we'd ask the other if he or she needed anything.

It was like a war. "I'm going down," we'd say to each other, knowingly. "…Want crackers?"

I left home, more or less, by 17. Before that I had been a chronic runaway for more than a year. And yet, as a young woman in my twenties I wanted to spend time with my mother. By then she was divorced and living in a sad, small condo about an hour away by train. I lived with a bunch of girls in an apartment and some weekends I just wanted a break from their constant primping and husband hunting. I'd take the train to my mothers and we'd spend all weekend watching old Hollywood movies.

Somewhere around 23, I began to realize that my mother was a little crazy, a little too weird. I got the idea that each time I saw her it was like I was exposing myself to a virus. I'd see her and feel terrible for days. At that time I lived in an apartment complex on the California Street cable car line. It had four pods of apartments around a large rectangular pool situated on the better part of a city block. There were two entrances (on the two opposite streets) both with heavy iron bars facing the streets and locked gates. Visitors had to be buzzed in.

When taking out garbage via an alleyway, one could see out to the street though the main fence without being seen. One night while taking out the garbage I was startled to see my mother there on the sidewalk with her back to the fence. She was crying into a hankie just outside my gate.

I stood frozen.

I expected to snap out of my shock and go to her but I just stood there holding my breath. I was afraid of her like I've never been afraid of anybody. I was Bambi coming up behind the hunter. It didn't matter to me what her drama was: who hurt her, beat her or rejected her. I think that was the moment of my initial adult emotional separation from my mother. That's when instinct overtook my emotional desire to have a mother; any mother. I backed up holding my garbage to my chest.

Q: How old were you when you first realized your mother was different than other mothers?

Because I grew up in a city, in a neighborhood where all the kids knew each other's homes as well as their own, by 8 or 9 I knew my mom was different. I felt that she was more concerned with her own life than being a mother. I knew she was out for herself.

Q: What is your biggest criticism of your mother?

As an adult I see that some of her damage, she couldn't help. But my main criticism of her is that she was unnecessarily cruel.

Q: What would she criticize about you?

When I cried she used to say, "Poor Rayne, you've got it so rough!" I know now that from her perspective my life was so much better — practically Rebecca of Sunnybrook Farm — compared to her childhood. She felt I had no reason to complain about anything.

Q: Describe any significant periods of estrangement. How easy (or difficult) was it to limit (or cut off) contact?

Beginning in my mid-20's I would avoid my mother for weeks or months at a time. When we did have contact she would know the exact date of our last conversation and remind me of it. It made me feel guilty and I'd try to check in more often to avoid it. But each time she'd pull the same thing so I figured I'd get the same verbal slap in the face whether I went a week or an entire summer, so the periods of no contact got longer and longer.

When I was 26 my mother crashed my first wedding, got drunk and made a fool of herself. She had to be carried out of the dining room by staff of the Awanhee Hotel in Yosemite National Park. It didn't embarrass me at all because I expected it. I had been upstairs trying to use the bathroom in a wedding dress. My girlfriend came in to warn me that my mother was being 86'd by the hotel staff. I just rolled my eyes. As I came down the stairs I got a glimpse of my mother's back. She was being carried out, lifted up off the floor by two staffers and her little feet were flicking back and forth an inch above the ground.

"Where did she put it all?" my dad wondered aloud. He said she had been drinking like a sailor with a hollow leg.

By then I had really separated her life and my life, so the reception continued. The morning after the wedding I found a wrapped box on the hood of my car. It was a photo album from my childhood. That was her weird wedding present to me — documentation of my great childhood.

The happier I was the easier it was to have no contact.

Even divorcing my first husband failed to trigger that mother need in me.

My second husband never met my mother.

She died unexpectedly in 2009 after a two-day hospitalization for pneumonia. I have no doubt that in the end my mother didn't want to see me because she didn't want to be seen as old and frail, gray and wrinkled, pulling a small oxygen tank behind her. In the last two years of her life I spoke to her a handful of times. She always initiated the calls. On our last conversation when I told her we hadn't spoken for most of two decades, she asked why.

"Because you were not a very nice mother," I said.

"Reeeeeeeealllllly?" she squeaked.

I didn't believe that she had forgotten all of her many sins against us. I distinctly remember thinking: That's interesting. She's trying to see if I'll believe that she is so old she's forgotten.

Q: How has your relationship with your mother affected your relationships with others?

I was a gregarious loner because I didn't trust people not to turn on me. I said I preferred men friends to women friends in general, but in truth I feared any woman who had any similar trait to my mother. I missed out on a lot of friendships because of it. I also tended to take a lot of bad treatment from men and suffer in silence. That's how I had coped since I was a kid.

Q: How many friends can you really talk to about your mother?

I always tell the truth about my mother if it comes up. I can tell anyone anything they want to know.

Q: Describe your current family status. Do you have children? If not, why not?

I have been happily married for nearly 20 years to an awesome man. We have no children by choice. Like a lot of daughters of toxic moms I consciously chose not to make babies thinking that I might let them down or hurt them. We dote on our dogs and enjoy theater, music and travel. We entertain a lot. We laugh a lot.

Q: Describe your current relationship with your mother. Given your current levels of contact how are you viewed within your family?

My adoptive mother is deceased. I'm writing about her with family support. My birth mother is alive and wants no contact with me. I'm her mistake. Her secret. My stepmother (my father's widow) lived 20 minutes away from us for the final eight years of her life. We loved her and looked out for her until she died in 2011 at the age of 89. She was a great lady.

Q: Have you ever talked to a therapist about your mother? Was it helpful?

What is amazing to me is that I never thought I needed to or could benefit from therapy. My father always feared therapists. He'd say if you feel like your head is scrambled go hug a tree; get out in nature.

It wasn't until I was severely stressed out at work and sought therapy that I learned that I could handle plenty of stress until some personal exchange triggered my mother's voice in my head belittling me. That voice could irrationally convince me I'd be fired; when it wasn't the case. Work stress could quickly morph into childlike fear of my mother coming at me, although I didn't really connect the dots without a therapist's help.

With therapy I was able to unearth and face long buried incidents. For example, there is a technique where the therapist has you hold your head still and you follow their finger or an object to the left and to the right with your eyes while describing a person or incident from your life. The idea is that you are re-thinking experiences using both your left and right brains, basically.

During one of those sessions I recalled my mother flipping my lip, knocking my head back and making me cry. Literally, I felt it in my therapist's office and reacted as if my mother was in the room hurting me. It startled my therapist, I think. I had forgotten or blocked out that regular form of humiliating punishment.

I later called my brother to make sure my memory was authentic and he confirmed that we both were regularly "flipped" in the face by our mother.

I had a very good therapist who gently lifted heavy weights off my shoulders. She helped me sort out fresh normal stress from old buried stress. She taught me to recognize when it kicked in and the difference between my own subconscious voice and my mother's voice on boxed wine. You know that voice, the one who says, "Who do you think you are, smarty pants?" I wish I had gone to therapy earlier.

Q: Moving forward, do you anticipate any changes in your view of your mother?

If I were writing fiction based on my mother, this would be much easier because the story would stay the same. I realize that no matter how much I bare my soul for this book, in the future my perception of my life might change a little as I continue to mature.

Hard to imagine now but I may be more forgiving at some point. I have been doing family history work on my mother's family and most everything I learn increases my understanding of her life. So changes in my view of my mother are inevitable.

She came from a fundamental Mormon family with lots of polygamy and old man/young girl stuff. Remember Warren Jeffs? The guy who liked 14-year-old-brides? Same family.

My mother and her mother/1930's

She also was kidnapped by her mother, (this is something I know about my mother that she herself did not know) who dragged her along on her own alcoholic and man binges. No doubt my mother had a hard life. But a lot of women do and they still manage to treat their children with love and respect.

Q: Do you experience personal guilt, social guilt or remorse about decisions you've made regarding your mother?

Not at all. My only regret is that I was not firmer about the early breaks. I wasted a lot of energy and emotion giving her chances to be a mother. The child in me always wanted a mother. Today I am my own mother in a weird way.

I try to be kind to myself and to take care of myself. It is still hard for me to accept kindness but I'm not afraid to let others mother me. I can accept kindness and concern in a healthy way now. I've even learned to ask for help, something I wasn't able to do for over 40 years.

Q: As your mother ages, do you see yourself having more or less contact? Why?

I never had plans to be there for my mother. My brother and I agreed that we would make phone calls or sign things for her as needed to make the end of her life easier, but neither of us would be driving her to appointments or checking on her physically. That was the right decision.

In 2009 my mother checked herself into a hospital for pneumonia and died two days later. It was very unexpected. A former smoker, she had COPD — trouble breathing — and used oxygen, so even a cold could have killed her, we were told.

The first day she went in her friend called my brother and he called me. We discussed whether one of us or both should travel to the hospital. But why, we debated. It wasn't like we could do anything positive for her. Plus we ran the risk of her saying or doing something that might haunt us.

My brother (the big softie) was leaning towards going but was really dreading it. At first I said I absolutely wouldn't go, but then I decided if he went I would, too. I didn't want him going by himself. Together we were stronger. Together we could make any of her outbursts comical. We agreed to sleep on it and I was resigned to going for him even going so far as planning time off from work.

The morning I learned my mother had died I was out on a story. I was a newspaper reporter and my brother called me just before I got out of my car to cover a small town fundraiser. It was a quaint event put on by ladies who donated knick-knacks, honey, jams that sort of thing for sale to raise money for some little non-profit.

It was a sunny day and I had parked on a dirt road under a shady tree. My cell phone rang. My brother said our mother had died the night before. I sat back down in the driver's seat and rolled down my window and listened to bees buzzing nearby for a long, long time.

Within minutes we had agreed that because he lived closer to her condo and had more freedom (he's not on the clock as I was on my job) that he would be the executor for the probate courts. My logic: every time we divided Halloween candy he always gave me my favorites and gave me extras.

I felt I could trust my brother.

After we hung up I sat there for a minute having that 'I'm nobody's kid anymore feeling wash over me. But then I snapped out of it and went to work.

The probate judge determined our mother died without a will and designated my brother as the executor with my sign-off. The probate took over a year. My brother worked his butt off, not only straightening out all her banking, investment and taxes issues, but he also cleaned out and sold her condo. On the day my brother visited me to write us each final checks granting us 50 percent of my mother's small estate I expected to be ecstatic.

I imagined I'd be jumping up and down and kissing that check. I had been working since 17 and had recently been collecting unemployment. When had I ever received a big bag of money? As my brother drove away all I could think was: Isn't it sad that she didn't want either of us to get a dime.

I told my husband what I felt and he said, "Think of it this way. You got a dime for every time she hurt you. Today was your payday. Be happy — you earned it."

Toxic Mom Toolkit
Book Club Questions

1. How would you define a toxic mother?

2. What could you do to help a young person who has a toxic mom?

3. What can you do when you learn that a friend is struggling with a toxic mother?

4. Do you think an adult can have living parents and still feel like an orphan?

5. What held your interest most, the author's memoir or the women's stories? Why?

6. Has anyone ever told you that they had a toxic mother? What was your reaction?

7. If you had a Toxic Mother could you have little contact or no contact with her? How would you manage that?

8. What story made you put the book down for a while?

9. How do different voices enhance the topic of toxic parenting?

10. What was the funniest story in the book?

11. What was the most heartbreaking story in the book?

12. What story or image in this book will you never forget?

13. Did the book end the way you expected?

14. Why do you think the author wrote this book?

15. Would you recommend the book to a close friend?

16. Rate this book from 1 to 5, with 5 being a strong/positive recommendation.

Toxic Mom Toolkit Community Volunteering:
Teaching sewing & mending to children
Can include after-school programs, Sunday Schools, detention facilities, or Scouting meetings.

Mending Syllabus

Today's Project:
Learning to mend by sewing small hearts as keepsakes, decorations or presents.

Definition of mending:
To restore something
to a satisfactory state.

Mending is never perfect, but it is what we do when we care about something and don't want to throw it away.

We can mend torn clothes and we can mend friendships and relationships.

The only thing required is a willingness to do so and patience.

Materials: Pre-cut red felt hearts, material hearts, embroidery thread, stuffing, buttons, red pipe cleaners (for hooks), and large embroidery needles.

Examples: Can include several finished hearts in different sizes and materials, vintage linens and books on embroidery for inspiration.

"Forgiveness is the needle that knows how to mend."
- Jewell

Toxic Mom Toolkit Reading List

*B*ecause you ARE good enough and the right book can get us through just about anything, I have compiled a short list of Toxic Mom Toolkit recommended books.

This list will always be changing and growing. Check Toxic MomToolkit.com for updates. If you have a book that helped you please let me know at Toxic Mom Toolkit on Facebook or at ToxicMomToolkit.com.

Horrible Mothers: Breach of a Sacred Trust by Alice Thie Viera Phd.

Will I Ever Be Good Enough?: Healing the Daughters of Narcissistic Mothers by Karyl McBride

Toxic Parents: Overcoming Their Hurtful Legacy and Reclaiming Your Life by Susan Forward and Craig Buck

Memoir: "House Rules" by Rachel Sontag

Daughter of the Queen of Sheba: A Memoir by Jacki Lyden

<u>When you and Your Mother Can't Be Friends: Resolving the Most Complicated Relationship of Your Life</u> by Victoria Secunda

<u>Mean Mothers: Overcoming the Legacy of Hurt</u> by Peg Streep

<u>Mama Drama: Making Peace with the One Woman Who Can Push Your Buttons, Make You Cry, and Drive You Crazy</u> by Denise McGregor

<u>Mothers Who Drive Their Daughters Crazy: Ten Types of Impossible Moms and How to Deal with Them</u> by Susan Simon Cohen and Edward M. Cohen

<u>The Mother I Carry: A Memoir of Healing from Emotional Abuse</u> by Louise M. Wisechild

<u>The New Don't Blame Mother: Mending the Mother-Daughter Relationship</u> by Paula Caplan

<u>Leaving Home: The Art of Separating From Your Difficult Family</u> by David P. Celani

<u>Emotional Blackmail: When the People in Your Life Use Fear, Obligation, and Guilt to Manipulate You</u> by Susan Forward

<u>Secret Daughter: A Mixed Race Daughter and the Mother Who Gave Her Away</u> by June Cross

<u>The Girl Nobody Wants</u> by Lily O'Brien

<u>Climbing the Broken Stairs: A Memoir</u> by Frieda Annette Adkins

<u>The New Orphan: When Parents Abandon their Adult Children</u> by Judith Clyde

<u>Mother, Stranger</u> by Cris Beam

<u>Why Me?</u> By Sarah Burleton

Author Note to Contributors

The "Voices" chapters are stories I've written based on the "20 Questions Every Adult Daughter of a Toxic Mother Should Ask Herself" questionnaires I received from women all over the world. Some submitters I've met, or spoken to on the phone and chatted via e-mail. When I could, I asked each submitter to read her pre-publication chapter. Unfortunately, some submitters became un-contactable during the three years it took to write this book.

I have changed identifying information, names, locations and other details to protect the identities of the women behind the Voices.

If I have not been able to tell you personally I want to tell you now that I am grateful for your participation. Toxic Mom Toolkit would not have been much of a book without your stories.

With Love,

Rayne

Journalist **Rayne Wolfe** lives in Petaluma, California, the
land of Happy Cows. She has been a business columnist
for the San Francisco Chronicle and Seattle Times ("What
Works") and spent a decade working as a regional reporter based in
Sonoma County for the New York Times system.

Her freelance articles and short stories have appeared in Chicken
Soup for the Gardener's Soul, BARK Magazine, the Miami Herald,
and Glamour Magazine, among others.

She volunteered as a law enforcement chaplain for five years and
currently writes a Food & Drink column for two newspapers.
She is married to a California Highway Patrol Lieutenant.
They have two dogs: Carmen, an English Bull
Terrier and Whiskey, a deaf Jack Russell Terrier.